Harry,

Alex

The World's Best Shoots

The World's Best Shoots

A Sporting Odyssey

Alex Brant

STACKPOLE
BOOKS

Dedicated to William C Steinkraus –
Sportsman, Bird shooter, 'Old African Hand',
Horseman, Olympic Gold Medallist, Author,
Editor, Musician, Great Friend –
The Last Renaissance Man.

First published in the UK in 2008
by Quiller, an imprint of Quiller Publishing Ltd

Published by
STACKPOLE BOOKS
5067 Ritter Road
Mechanicsburg, PA 17055
www.stackpolebooks.com

ISBN 978-0-8117-0441-0

Printed in China

Contents

Foreword

While the title *World's Best Shoots* is appropriate, a better one might have been *Alex Brant's Favourite Shoots*. For one thing, I have not been to every shoot in the world (although I am now heading into my forty-ninth season of sport so I have done a few); and also the word 'best', at least in this case, must be slightly subjective. Indeed, I have not used best only to imply difficulty, which is certainly one criterion. Personally, I would rather shoot one bird well that stretches my abilities than numerous birds that, while still testing and challenging, are not memorable. But within these constraints it must also be acknowledged that all shooters are not created equal. While I am often complimented on my shooting, I know in my heart of hearts that I am not a George Digweed or a Richard Faulds. Difficult or challenging birds cannot be the sole criterion. In this book I have tried to pick shoots that would either challenge the best shooters in the world – for example, the toughest drives at Castle Hill, North Molton, Whitfield or La Cuesta – and other shoots that provide challenging birds for the good normal shot who is not a high bird expert. (High birds require specialized guns that can handle heavy loads without overly debilitating the man behind the weapon, i.e. a heavyish gun and tight chokes.) Not every shot enjoys this aspect of our sport and there is as much to be said for a good day on sporting birds in the 30–40 yard range that can be cleanly and humanely dispatched with a pair of beautiful, relatively lightweight shotguns and appropriate cartridges, these firearms often handed down from generation to generation.

There are enough great shoots for a four-volume set to make this complete and exhaustive. Certainly, there are another thirty to fifty pheasant and partridge shoots in Great Britain worthy of discussion; another three or four Spanish shoots; ptarmigan in Scotland and Snake Valley chuckars are unique experiences for fit sportsmen; pigeon in Bolivia or Paraguay; mixed bag shoots in Uruguay…you get the idea. Fortunately, I was not asked to be encyclopaedic.

In addition to the aspect of difficulty, there is also the aspect of conviviality. Does the shoot organization have a collegial feel to it? Is the food good? Are the toilets clean? Is the wine superior, if you are paying top dollar? Is the house or the estate historic or otherwise interesting? All of these factors and others go in to making a best shoot.

I have done my best to try and convey both a sense of time and place and to accurately describe both the shooting and the organization. The further one travels from home, the more important the quality of the organization. It makes no sense to travel halfway round the world only to discover on arrival that firearm paperwork has not been completed as required. Every shoot that I have recommended does a first class job of arranging local transport, gun permits, hunting licences, etc. (Do realize that it is *your responsibility* to provide the shoot operator with all the necessary details so that the necessary licences can be completed in *sufficient* time.)

Before I go further, I must thank my friends who have graciously supplied chapters. They are, alphabetically: Mike Barnes, Jose Pepe Fanjul, Majid Jafar, John McCloy II, Richard Purdey, Clinton Smullyan, Don Terrell, and Vic Ventors. I must also profoundly thank Peter Johnson, David Perez, Steve Thomas and Nancy Whitehead for their outstanding photographs, which they generously provided.

Many of these chapters first appeared in magazines in a modified form. I thank the editors and publishers for their permission to reproduce the articles, especially Will Hetherington of the *Shooting Gazette* who supplied the professional photos that ran with the Stratfield Saye, Molland and Highclere articles; plus La Flamenca and Chargot, which Renata and I photographed.

Pinos Altos, Las Golondrinas, Casa de Campo plus a modified version of Ireland first appeared in *Shooting Sportsman*, as did Vic Ventors' piece on The Ledges.

Fieldsports published my story on Argentine Dove and Mike Barnes's Whitfield story.

Shooting Gazette ran my features on Stratfield Saye, Ballywalter, Highclere, Chargot and La Flamenca plus a different version of Ireland, and Duck in Argentina.

Sports Afield first published La Cuesta – The World's Best Tall Partridge Shoot.

All chapters not given attribution are by yours truly.

Most stories have been changed or updated. North Molton, Castle Hill, Haddeo, Prescombe and many other reviews are new.

Whether your main area of interest is chasing woodcock behind pointers or spaniels, shooting driven game or wildfowling, I hope that this book will lead you to a great adventure and an experience of a lifetime.

My booking agency can best be viewed at www.drivenshooting.com

Introduction

Anyone writing a tome that purports to be a listing of 'the world's' best shoots, must know that they are on course to attract a few critics. It is essentially an impossible task, but if anyone can pull it off it is Alex.

An American by birth, and a hunter by instinct, Alex Brant has spent practically all of his sixty years travelling the world in search of quality sport. And as he grew older his special passion became driven game, to such an extent that he and his delightful (and very sporting) partner Renata Coleman took on Humewood Castle, which Renata owned, in Ireland to develop it into a fantasy shoot of their own. From modest beginnings, and equally modest mallard, eventually Alex was able to deliver the kind of fabulous duck shooting that matched the billing of the couple's wonderful home and estate.

A couple of years ago they upped sticks and moved to the north of Scotland. Along the way he has spent practically every spare hour either planning shooting, writing about shooting, travelling to shoots, and most importantly actually pulling the trigger.

He even started his own sporting agency in order that he could both make good use of his experience and also take parties to destinations around the world where he had found sport at its very best.

So his book takes us from North and South America, to African countries, Eastern Europe and Spain, the latter being a country offering the kind of sport of which he is very fond. But most particularly he is passionate about the kind of shooting to be found in the UK. He does not in fact list the world's best shoots – as he quite rightly points out, he writes about the best shoots that he has been to. Many famous estates are included, and many omitted – for instance there are no pheasant shoots listed from Yorkshire and only one from Wales (I must speak to him about this – he doesn't know what he's missing). And with the erratic English weather and the unpredictable nature of game shooting, it is impossible to judge a shoot from a single visit. In fairness, most included here are reported from a depth of experience. But there are odd exceptions, Chargot being one – Chargot has been a tremendously consistent performer over the years, and a great flag bearer for West Country shooting. I would urge a revisit.

But with Alex you get what he sees. And for that you always have a full-value read. He is very knowledgeable on guns, ballistics and the sport – added to which he writes with great irony, as well as honesty, which makes for a great combination. He also never minds talking about himself in a way that might, to British sensitivities, appear boastful. Referring to shooting seventeen pheasants without missing, all first barrel, he expresses disappointment that five were hit in the middle and not the front end! From others this might sound conceited but from Alex it's just the way it was.

He has a good way with words (as many of us have seen from his musings in various magazines) and a rich seam of amazing contacts. In this book he entertainingly writes of his visits to a number of Britain's finest shoots. He takes us behind the scenes, we meet the hosts, sit at their dinner tables, and sample some of the finest pheasant shooting to be found anywhere in the world.

He is a first division Shot who holds his own in distinguished company, so he also writes as an end user, and is able to properly describe a day's shooting, the challenge involved and as an aside deliver invaluable tips for us lesser mortals. Most of all this is a very entertaining read – which coming from Alex Brant is just what you might expect. He seldom disappoints.

Mike Barnes
Fieldsports

Part I – Spain

Classic Spanish Partridge at Pinos Altos

I first shot in Spain nearly thirty-five years ago. I was a sophomore at McGill, not yet twenty, when I travelled to Madrid for a winter break. The Madrid Ritz was very different then. Very underused. Very proper. One would not dream of going to the lobby in less than a blue blazer and tie. I suppose it was off-season but rooms were only $12.00 and suites with separate sitting rooms were eighteen bucks. (This was before the hyperinflation of the 1970s.) Multitudes of uniformed staff attended to one's every need. Only the finest linens were used and if one left one's room for even fifteen minutes beds would be remade and shoes re-polished.

I had come for the pigeon shooting at Somontes, the great club, indeed Mecca, within Madrid. And it was spectacular shooting especially with the specifically bred zurito – the pigeon that is all wings, a small body and flies like a rocket.

The famous restaurants of the day – Horchers and The Jockey Club – were fabulous as well. I arrived at the Jockey at 10 pm, thinking I was pretty cool, in the way that a nineteen-year-old would on his first trip abroad, only to be told by the captain that I was most welcome to have a drink at the bar but that dinner was not served for another hour. Great red-legged partridge shooting was available near Madrid, all wild birds, and again the cost was not a significant factor.

In the early 1980s, I shot stag and deer with Juan Antonio Conde and Ricardo Medem at Cazatur's El Castano not too far from Toledo. I shot partridge at a great wild bird shoot in the west of Spain, Extremadura, based at the town of Trujillo, an ancient walled city. Within these walls stood a great palace restored and refurbished, if memory serves, by a member of the Whitney clan. It was here that Fernando Saiz (Nano) and Fernando Bustamante, then partners, housed their clients and guests. The accommodation was great, the food and wine spectacular, and the sport even better.

Fernando Saiz and Fernando Bustamante were then, and are now, both elegant gentlemen and sportsmen of the first order. A handshake was as good as a contract. Their partridge were totally wild. Certainly small groups of birds did come over, but early in the season it was primarily coveys, true family groups. However, times have changed and the massive predator controls that used to be acceptable, including strong indiscriminate poisoning, which enabled the commercial shooting of wild birds, has been banned. Reared partridge, if released properly when they are young, fly exceptionally well and prove a significant test for the skill of most guns. (I am not extolling the virtues of late releases, or crated birds, both of which practices occur and are deplorable.) The better shoots are a combination of wild and reared perdiz, though wild birds are in the minority.

The pleasures of partridge shooting are great. Though a true Spanish line, with guns vying for bragging rights on the drive or the day, can be quite competitive, for foreign teams this is not normally part of the equation. The ambience of the day afield is much like a day in the British Isles, but somehow more relaxed, more inviting. And the weather is so much better. The British Isles often have rain coming in horizontally. In Britain, on a few days, I have been known to skip lunch, opting instead to dry and clean my guns.

I have had the great good fortune to shoot with Fernando Saiz at Pinos Altos. The estate is located about two hours from Madrid, reached by skirting Toledo and then heading south on good roads. This is La Mancha country. A land where fighting bulls are bred, olives are grown and Spanish oaks are common.

The estate had been an inheritance from Nano's grandfather almost twenty-five years ago. Nano knows the property intimately, having hunted there since he was quite young. It has been in his family since the sixteenth century, when the current farmhouse was built. Obviously, it has been renovated more than once.

There are two main areas of the estate. The first, contiguous to the main house, is primarily for big-game hunting and offers great sport for red stag, fallow deer and other species. The second is a ten-minute drive away and is exclusively for partridge shooting. The partridge side of the property is nearly

6,000 acres. It is a rough, stark landscape interspersed with many small and large hills, olive groves, a stream and other features that result in a diverse ecosystem just to the liking of the red legs. They have shot perdiz at Pinos Altos for about a decade. Nano had prepared the property for two or three years before accepting clients. He is no newcomer to the profession, however, having twenty-five years' experience outfitting big-game hunters and organizing first-class partridge shoots.

Upon my arrival at Pinos Altos, Clara a young, petite and attractive girl comes to my room to take the guns to the safe. I offer to help, she balks; I insist and prevail. I cannot picture her lugging both pairs in their cases.

'Do you wish to shoot four guns? I can get you a second loader.' (I brought two pairs because I did not trust the triggers on one pair of Famars aka Abbiatico and Salvinelli; unfortunately, I was correct in my pessimism.)

'It's not a problem,' she insists.

You have to love a country where shooting a trio or a quartet is common-place. But I did not want to be or appear greedy, as I knew the rest of the line would only be shooting pairs. (The trio can be shot with one or two loaders – a quartet requires two.) My loader, Paco, was the best I've ever had and so quick that he was usually behind in sequence only two or three times a day and then just for a couple of seconds, so a trio would have been of marginal added utility. (Was Paco so fast or was I so much slower than the legendary Spanish shots?)

Each year Fernando Saiz keeps one week for a mixed team of guns. While our team was heavily weighted to Texans, an Argentine now living in Florida and two noble Spaniards, husband and wife, completed our team. (I later learned that Clara was their daughter. The love for hunting in Spain is often genetic.)

The King is a frequent visitor to the shoot. He was here the week before shooting with General Norman Schwarzkopf. '41' often shoots on this team. President Bush wrote an article that was reprinted in one of the English newspapers, *The Mail on Sunday*, in which he extolled the virtues of shooting and fishing. He did, however, warn against being placed in a butt between the General and Juan Carlos. He felt that they were such good shots that it made it too difficult for the man in the middle. 'Every time I'd aim, guns would sound on either side of me, feathers would fly and birds would drop. I got a few but my shooting mates wiped my eye every time.' Fortunately, or unfortunately, most of us will never have to worry about that. He was, of course, talking about the shooting at Pinos Altos.

Highlights of Each Day

Day one

The first drive started a little behind schedule due to, of all things, fog; a rare occurrence in Iberian shooting. It lingered slightly during the first drive causing the birds to fly a bit lower than usual making them an even more challenging target. (A low pheasant is a bore, but perdiz are a bird of a different feather. Just like grouse, and *no one* asks for tall grouse, one does not have to have them at least thirty-five yards up to enjoy good sport as one does with pheasant.) The way they fly naturally creates all the sport one could wish. A low, fast bird that often changes his line is tricky indeed. The recent phenomenon of making them fly over ravines to mimic pheasant, while providing good sport, or in the case of La Cuesta *fantastic sport*, can be somewhat artificial. It is occurring as a secondary effect of the current fashion for tall pheasant and led by English lines and English agents. My own view is that one should enjoy both classic partridge and tall partridge but not dismiss true Spanish shooting at its best. If I had to only choose one, it would be the classic shooting. Luckily both are available and, indeed, can be combined on one trip.

Sky under the bird is one of the keys to safe shooting.

Because of the fog it is impossible to see the line of beaters. We are told we can shoot low in front until the flags appear. (Each of the thirty-five or so beaters uses and carries a flag atop his ten-foot pole: white for the ordinary team, national flags on the end, the yellow flag for each of three gamekeepers controlling the line – quite a colourful spectacle. From that time on we can shoot medium or tall birds in front as long as there is sufficient sky around each partridge.)

The others, we can take behind. The lingering fog made it difficult to see the birds until they were within range. Quick reflexes were a must. Great shooting, although I probably killed a third of my birds behind. The land itself is largely scrub, with plenty of rocks and some oaks, the acorns of which give the Spanish ham such a distinctive and delicious flavor.

I am in the left *punta*. (*Punta* means end position in Spanish.) The Marquis de Laula is on my right and we are on a path on a hillside surrounded by trees. Birds that come in high are straightforward enough but still quite a challenge. Those that come in low through the breaks in the scrub and trees are very tough from my peg. Think of a low eight at skeet where brush obscures the first half of the target's flight. Birds are taken in front, low, on the sides and behind. There are great tall birds at the other side of the line. The birds on the right, where the slope is greatest, transmute from partridge to teal as they make the turn to the right over the line. Variety prevails.

Lunch is served in an old, refurbished farmhouse on this part of the estate, perhaps fifteen minutes from the main house. The food is wonderful and the service impeccable. The large living room, with big sofas and a roaring fireplace, adds to the ambience. After three drives we've made the bag. The team votes to call it quits rather than go to overage. The wine and food, both excellent, flow. The last drive of the day is a siesta.

The evening starts with cocktails. As always, Nano and Koki are perfect hosts. We drink and chat in the hall where Nano's trophies from Africa hang high overhead. It is appropriate. Four big-game hunters are also in the group, though shooting a different part of the estate for stag and fallow deer. Some have already shot ibex in Gredos or Ronda. All are happy.

The house is a large, classic Spanish house built around a courtyard that has been in Nano's family for ages. When Nano inherited it, he, being a talented architect by training, remodelled and refurbished it. All the bedrooms were outstanding. Tremendous thought was given to the requirements of the shooters and their companions and it can be seen in all the details down to the design of the closets. The rooms are both charming and comfortable and each shooter is assured a great deal of pampering. The view from the veranda is spectacular. Stags serenade.

Habanas are smoked on the large terrace. Stags, because of the mild fall, are still roaring. Had it been socially acceptable, I would have roared too. The clocks moved back an hour providing more time in the arms of Morpheus. All is peaceful.

Day two

The second day is bright and clear and the shooting starts right on schedule. On the first drive I'm in the middle, the heart of the action. Unfortunately, there is a tree the size of the Statue of Liberty right in front of me. I have no warning until the birds appear just a few yards away – there is often no time to mount. The only way to shoot the birds coming at me at low or moderate height is behind. I finally accept this.

This is followed by the best drive of the day, called Chinatal. The Marquis de Laula comes over to me. He is dapperly dressed in a tweed shooting vest and matching breeks. He tells me where he is positioned. Again I am in a *punta*, this time at the right end of the line, which is shaped like an L, with yours truly being at the bottom right. *Pantallas* (metal plates on poles) are put out on every drive to prevent one from being shot by one's neighbour or shooting another Gun. Since we cannot really see each other it is impossible to place them accurately. But there is a forest between us for thirty-five yards and I doubt a pellet would get through, although I admire his caution. Driven shooting can be very dangerous. Shooting glasses with side protection are a must. I can see great numbers of birds coming off the hillside more than half a mile away. The flushing points must be large as the birds leave the top in *barras*, though they tend to split into two or three groups before they arrive at the guns. (A *barra* is a large group of perdiz, like a bouquet of pheasant or twenty coveys of quail.) Many birds pass on my right out of range, though I am able to connect with a few long crossers. Some very tall birds come over, which is great fun and very amusing as a Spaniard would say. Long crossers, some straight at one's face, and birds best taken behind all provide unique challenges. The shooting is fast and furious and for the only time in the three days a trio would be handy. Forty-four birds are on my clicker, ninety so far for the day. Life is very good. It is a beautiful day. Sunny and so warm that I switch from an Austrian chapeau to one made of straw from Lock's of London. (I have driven from the British Isles – obviously a ferry was used for part of the safari – so my car is very well equipped for any emergency from minor gun repairs to an urgent need for sloe gin or Habanas.)

At lunch, I presume the day is over so I consume two or three glasses of *vino tinto*. 'You have no complaints,' one of the Guns says to me. 'I don't think anyone has heard me complaining,' I say with a smile and I mean it.

The Spanish mentality is for everyone to know how everyone else shot on each and every drive. That way they can joke and tease each other. Personally I don't think it's always a good idea, especially for foreign guns. Someone shoots a hundred cartridges and feels great until he learns that he only accounted for twelve birds in the bag. Fairness, if there is such a thing, is in giving everyone roughly the same amount of shooting (i.e. cartridges fired); ability then determines the individual's bag. Indeed, I've often seen great shots draw bad pegs and still kill double the team average. More power to them. Just don't rub it in.

Nano announces it is time for the last drive of the day. He is very generous and he hates charging overage unless the bag is very large, but he doesn't mind too terribly going five or ten per cent extra for the day. 'Alex is allowed to shoot how many birds?' Renata mischievously queries. Nano, without missing a beat, replies 'one', a big grin on his face.

To make good on his word I am placed on the far left of the line, high on the hillside. Today the line is small, only five. The manager always places the Guns in order to make it good, fair shooting for everyone. He excelled. The birds to the far right of the line are extraordinary. As the partridge break cover they go straight up and to make it more extreme the land slopes away from them to the line below. The majority of birds are very good but killable at forty yards. Some are the equal of English archangel pheasant at sixty yards. It is glorious to watch. And while I'm a bit out of it, I still manage to break a hundred. I light a cigar. And as I do, like Sherlock Holmes with a three-pipe problem, I reflect: this is partridge as it should be, driving the bird in its native habitat, allowing it to fly as it chooses, depending on topography, wind and mood.

Day three

On the third and final day we shoot on the opposite side of the road over very different terrain. Here the hills slope upward at about 30°. The Guns were either placed along wide fire breaks on the hillside, which is covered in low brush, or on the field below in front of a large olive grove. The birds were driven horizontally across the hillside with flagmen on a long line above the beaters running the entire length from the beaters' line, almost a mile away to the fire-break on which the Guns stood.

Partridge tend to fly two or three times before encountering the Guns. The first time or two when pushed they just fly a few hundred yards before settling. The last time they may fly a mile or even more. (This last journey exhausts them and they need at least twenty minutes to recover before they can fly again.)

At the top of the team, I have the lion's share of the shooting early, although it tapers off as the drive progresses. My early birds are high and the Guns in the field, again, had a lot of tall partridge.

After this drive, we had an early break for tapas to give the birds a chance to rest as they were going to be driven back from the other direction. There's more than one way to describe the action of driving birds back and forth but I prefer Nano's Spanish term *cara y cruz*, meaning heads and tails (literally heads and crosses as the verso of a Spanish coin is a cross). The Cruz part of this double drive gave me a fair number of very low birds behind, and for the first time this shot, which is fairly uncomfortable for me, started to work consistently. The key, it seemed, was to shoot even lower. Easier said than done on birds that are only two or three feet above the ground and dropping. Most missed shots were over the top.

Lunch was back at the farmyard just across the road. Pre-lunch drinks were served, as usual, by uniformed, attentive staff.

The afternoon was basically a repeat of the wonderful morning. We were farther downhill, perhaps a mile or so to the right of the firebreak shot earlier. Again, the birds were shot horizontally across the hillside, and many curling high birds, towering towards the heavens, showed for the Guns in front of the olive trees.

As we had earlier, we took a break between the drives to give the birds plenty of time to rest and recover their strength before the return drive.

I am a lucky man. I get to do what I love and call it a profession. I have many great days each year shooting at some of Britain's top ten shoots and travel for sport to Africa or South America most years as well. But I always look forward to my days in Spain. The Spanish are a great sporting people, the climate is sublime and strong-flying partridge provide great and unique challenges to be treasured.

Some general, random thoughts: the Spaniards are very competitive. In the old days, *secretarios*, with or without prodding from their Guns, would often cheat by stealing their neighbour's birds. (Betting was involved.) Today at most commercial shoots the clicker rules. *Secretarios* keep count and on some shoots announce each *perdiz* killed as it happens. The Gun, remaining silent, accepts the count but he can correct the number if he judges that his neighbour killed the bird in question or he can add a bird that the *secretario* did not see him hit. The rough terrain frequently encountered these days lends to the greater accuracy of the counter.

In Spain, everyone knows who the great shots are. At one time Count Teba with 448 to his own gun on one day was tops. Juan Abello Gallo was generally considered the top gun until recently. Now the familiar name, grandson not reincarnation, is Francisco Franco. He is considered the king of shooting. He uses five guns with unerring precision. Let us not forget King Juan Carlos who shoots frequently, usually arriving by military helicopter. He usually shoots a quartet.

His own shoot, La Encomienda de Mudela, is not too far away. It is strictly a wild bird shoot and according to my friend, Pepe Fanjul, who has shot as a guest of the King a number of times, it is quite spectacular with very large daily bags. To keep the quality and the quantity high, King Juan Carlos only shoots it a few days – these days can be counted on the fingers of one hand – each season.

Tapas are an integral aspect of each day. Good Rioja, Spanish ham (as addictive, I presume, as most drugs), cheese and other goodies – all fattening – are normally served after the second or third drive.

Shooting Partridge

Not everyone who shoots in Spain brings a pair of guns and this is a mistake according to Beltran, the manager of the partridge shoot and a partner in the company. 'You just cannot kill enough birds with one gun.' (The sole exception was my good friend and great shot Gary Herman who shot here with one gun the previous season and was high gun every day. There are only so many Gary Hermans and even fewer George Digweeds in this world.) While it is preferable that the pair is matched, according to Beltran, at least they should be close and for god's sakes make sure that they are the same gauge. (Some Guns have arrived in Spain with one 12 and one 20. Smart, real smart!)

The greatest mistake, according to Nano, is that most foreigners shooting Spanish partridge wait too long to fire the first barrel. 'Use a modified choke and kill the first perdiz way in front. Shoot the second quickly as well.' That allows one time to switch guns and shoot two more in front. If one waits for the first bird until it is too close, all the rest will have to be taken behind. (To be effective and efficient with double guns one must train oneself to look to the front during the switch over.)

If you haven't shot partridge before, the following drill should prove helpful. You need access to a skeet field on your own. Practise incomers first from stations two and three and five and six. Work on breaking them early. Halfway from the opening to the stake is about right. Closer to the house is better. Get a feel for working the tip of your barrel as you mount the gun so that when the gun reaches your cheek the work is actually done. Move, mount and shoot: just fire and follow through. Next try this from stations one and seven, again working on killing the target as soon as you see it. The final exercise is to go to station eight. Start from the normal position, but then go forward a foot or two at a time. It goes without saying, but I'll say it anyway, that this entire programme is practised with a low gun. Now for the interesting part and why you really want to do this on your own. Using stations two and three and six and seven shoot the house you're closest to as a going away clay with your body set up facing away from the target (towards the near house). In other words, you are practising taking clay behind as you would a perdiz. Proper footwork is the key.

The Birds

The various operators use different methods of releasing partridge. Some, including Nano Saiz, release the birds when they are very, very young. They are placed in large pens to protect them from predators. As soon as they are capable of flying they are released. A number of estates, including some of the very good ones, release partridge that are a bit older and this is fine if done correctly. These tend to be released from small holding pens where they are kept for a few days to settle in. A percentage of the group is released thereafter each day and after a week all the birds are in the wild. The idea here is that the birds in the pen act as callbacks and keep the freshly released birds in the area while they find food and water. Some operators put out hoppers to feed the birds, while others primarily spin lines of wheat that are cast from four-wheel drives or quad bikes.

The only real problem associated with released birds, be it partridge in Spain or pheasant in the British Isles or on the Continent, are the operators who continue to put out birds throughout the season. These 'topped up' birds, often shot before they have had time enough to harden to the elements, prove less than testing targets. This is neither fair to the bird nor the shooter. The best shoots release all birds close to the same time, months before shooting begins.

Pure wild bird shoots are now a rarity. A handful of private shoots can accomplish this as they are only looking to shoot a few days in the season, and do not have the pressure to fill an agreed upon specific bag that has been paid for in advance by paying clients. The best of the commercial shoots are a combination of wild and reared birds. In some cases, in a good year, when the weather conditions are perfect and magpie numbers low, a substantial number of the birds will be wild. I doubt that this is ever a 50/50 equation these days on most commercial shoots. (There is an excellent operator who has formed a consortium of farmers near Jerez, the wild bird bastion of Spain, to provide about thirty days of sport early in the season.) And I must admit that some of this 'arithmetic' is guesswork on my part based on off-the-record conversations with at least half a dozen of the best Spanish shoots. But unless one is there working and seeing birds released, there is a combination of conjecture and research and trust tempered with my experience from years of raising tens of thousands of duck and pheasant on my own shoots. On a number of Spanish shoots one will see a lot of twigs placed on the ground as miniature huts called *chozo* to protect the birds from aerial predators and the heat of the noonday sun. This, to me, displays a shoot where birds are put out very early. (It also protects wild birds on barren terrain.) The different shoots release different numbers of birds as well. Some, like Las Golondrinas, tend to release the number of birds that are killed the previous season to help them keep a constant number of birds to show the Guns.

Remeter is the blanking in of large areas, often by horseback. Partridge are, unlike pheasant, not on the Pavlovian feed schedule or whistle. So they are pushed away (*remeter*) from the *querencia* (where they want to be, sort of like the home wood to a pheasant) and then driven back over the line of Guns towards the *querencia*. Horses are particularly good at breaking up a *barra*.

Although grouse in Scotland, with a good strong tailwind, or a curling archangel pheasant fifty-five yards overhead are more difficult to hit, the sheer variety of birds presented makes partridge shooting at the great Spanish shoots perhaps the most enjoyable of all. Birds may be taken in front, or to the sides as low, medium or tall crossers. A bird may not be seen because of the terrain or natural obstacle such as the tree or rock in time to be taken in front and will have to be taken behind. High birds are straightforward, low are very tough targets. An incomer at eye level or lower suddenly seeing the line as he clears the final tree line sits on his tail like an F-16 and goes straight to the heavens. Indeed, I saw a number of archangel partridge inevitably at the other side of the line forty, fifty, or even sixty yards up. This is classic Spanish shooting with perdiz as tall birds because that is what they chose, not solely because a terrain of ravines dictates their flight.

The Partridge of Las Golondrinas

I first shot perdiz over twenty years ago with Fernando Bustamante and Nano Saiz near the town of Trujillo in western Spain. Guests were housed in an enormous manor within the old walled city. The shooting was strictly for wild birds, and it was all done over relatively flat land, although the Guns would often be placed in front of small hills to protect the beaters as much as to alter the presentation of the birds. Low birds taken well in front were the norm.

Fernando Bustamante is a particularly great sportsman, in a land of great sportsmen. He is very straightforward; his word is his bond. From an ancient Conquistador family, he would be too old fashioned for words except that he has a mischievous sense of humour and is always quick to deploy it. My final driven shoot one year came at the end of February, nearly a quarter of a century after first shooting with Fernando Bustamante. They legally shoot Extremadura until 8 March. It found me once again at his famed Las Golondrinas shoot.

It is located in the province of Extremadura in the west of Spain, roughly halfway between the towns of Caceres and Trujillo. This old family *finca*, once used for testing fighting bulls, is called Santa Cristina. Surrounding this old refurbished *finca* and farmyard lies 44,000 acres of typical traditional partridge land. Las Golondrinas is named for a black and white swallow with a forked tail that never seems to land, taking insects out of the air in the same fashion that we would take partridge – on the wing. Extremadura is named because it is a land of extremes, especially the weather, which varied while we were there from bright, warm sunshine to an amazing, though thankfully brief, hailstorm.

This is more the land of Spanish oaks than of olive trees, although of course the latter do exist in this area. Indeed, one of the most interesting shoots I have ever enjoyed was shooting olive thrush with Fernando twenty-five years earlier. We drove to a farmer's olive grove where we stood among the trees and shot these naturally decoying and passing birds. The birds were tiny, if memory serves about the size of a jacksnipe. One needed to use size 8 or 9 shot just so that they would not be able to fly through the pattern. And just as I have fond memories of olive trees for this obvious reason, I also have fond memories of the Spanish oak. My favourite ham in the world is that of Spain. One of the reasons it is so flavourful is that the pigs are allowed to munch the acorns, which give them their distinctive taste. On another trip to Spain last year, my better half, Renata, and I chose to drive starting with a ferry to France and head south from there. Soon after we arrived in San Sebastian, we walked from our hotel, the Mary Christina, to a typical Basque region bistro. The ham was brilliant.

But my main reason for stopping in San Sebastian was not for ham. It was to visit the gun companies. One of the three that I wanted to see was the Garbi factory in Eibar. We had our appointment and took the highway to the sprawling city. Although we had directions, we were quickly lost. No one that I know speaks Basque other than the local inhabitants. Luckily Renata does speak a bit of Spanish and we found a policeman. She asked him for directions. He said we would never find Garbi as it could only be reached by following an intricately linked system of one-way streets. Kindly and generously he offered to lead the way on his motorcycle. He was dead right. Left to our own devices, we would still be stuck in the maze of streets. (I was, by the way, a fool for not buying a pair of 28s since at the time a Euro could have been bought for about 85 cents in US$, making a pair extremely reasonable. And while a pair of Spanish guns does not have the panache of the English best, or the breathtaking engraving of the better Italian guns, they do have one attribute that at this stage of my life I tend to value above all the rest: they do work. I have recently purchased a pair of Garbis at auction.)

My group for Las Golondrinas was large, but then, too, was the expected bag of 800 perdiz per day. My co-captain for the three days of shooting red legs was Colonel Dennis Behrens, an ex-army guy from Texas. We first met a number of years ago. We hit it off immediately and he brought an entire team to our Humewood Castle shoot in Ireland. This time Dennis brought five friends and clients to shoot with him. Also joining us were two Irishmen who have lived in England for years and years. A New Zealander on his round-the-world retirement safari joined us for the first day only and when he left his spot was taken over by the only true Englishmen in the group. We came from the far ends of the English-speaking world, and we all came to shoot.

While all were very experienced Guns, only two other members had shot

Spanish partridge before. An Englishman new to this game, Graham Moore, told me how much the lie of the land reminded him of grouse shooting. I think he was actually stunned at the quality of the birds presented. At the end of the two days, he told me it was the best partridge shoot he had ever been on, and the final drive of the last day was the best partridge drive he had ever experienced.

As the shoot is located two and a half hours from Madrid, it is much better to stay the night after the last day's shoot and depart the next morning in time to catch one's flight home or for a day or two in the lovely capital city. Staying an extra night is certainly no hardship. After all, the food and accommodation is top drawer. Indeed, the food is under the direction of a cordon bleu chef who just happens to be Fernando's sister.

The part of the house that the shooting guests occupy is based around a long hallway that must stretch for about a hundred feet. Off this hallway are placed a dozen bedrooms (each with private bath), Fernando's office and the dining room. The tall walls stretching the entire length of the hallway are covered in Fernando's trophies from four continents. Indeed, with an estate as large as his, he could provide many more commercial days than he does. However, he does not want to let commercial shooting get in the way of his own sport. Between safaris in Africa, stag hunting and bird shooting in Argentina, grouse shooting in England and partridge to his own gun in Spain, Fernando shoots a hundred days a year. What a guy.

Daylight lasts much longer at this latitude than it does further north in the British Isles. The pace, ergo, is quite leisurely. Unless one drives to a far part of the estate, the morning journey is minimal. As we approached the shooting area, the ground was littered as it were with *chozo*, little teepee-shaped wooden huts designed for the partridge to run into to escape avian predators or the hot noon-day sun.

I was in the far *punta* at the right end of the line on the first drive of the first day. It was a bit of a hike for an old guy like me with a bad back, or at least it would have been had I been carrying my own guns and cartridges. Shooters in Spain are given a *cargador* and a *secretario*. The job of the first man is to be one's loader and of the second to count birds and remember or mark where they have gone down. It is also the job of these two gentlemen to carry all of the gear plus a pair or trio of guns and the cartridges.

The birds in general were classic traditional Spanish partridge. In other words, they flew low.

Low birds have a bad reputation, especially in Great Britain, for not providing sufficiently challenging sport. (The two exceptions for a Brit are red grouse, and wild grey partridge shot after they are pushed over hedgerows.) While this is a reasonable view with pheasants, perdiz can generally be relied upon, assuming they have been properly reared, to provide good sport at any height.

This is especially true if one shoots them the way a Spaniard does: *quickly*. They take the first two way in front, switch the guns with their loader and rapidly take two more. Waiting and just shooting one overhead partridge is too easy for the experienced driven game shot. But shooting it like a Spaniard is challenge enough for anyone. If you shoot them fast, half on the first barrel is ideal with quarter right for the second shot. Quarter and cylinder or cylinder and cylinder or quarter and quarter would be best in gun number two.

Sometimes, of course, one shoots what one has. A long time ago I stopped in Madrid for a couple of days of pigeon shooting at Club Somontes before heading on to England for some super tall pheasants at Lord Bledsoe's Cotswold estate where no team going back to Ripon beat one bird for three shots. I brought very tightly choked guns with me for obvious reasons. Out of the blue, I was invited for a day of partridge. While I did kill my share of birds, with this much choke some looked as though they had been breasted out with a dull penknife – not exactly seemly. (Actually I did quite well in the pigeon ring on a very informal day. My good friend Eduardo Araoz was with me and he made quite a bit of money betting on my behalf. I was just jet-lagged enough that I killed too many of my early birds with my second barrel. Eduardo got very good odds. When it was over, we were accused of sandbagging, which we had not.)

Classic partridge, like dove, do not need heavy loads to bring them down humanely. 24 grams (⅞ths of an ounce) is certainly sufficient in 12-gauge; 1 ounce should be the max. Often as not, I see 32-gram (1⅛ oz) loads used in Spain – a very macho land. As it is reasonable to shoot 200 to 500 rounds a day, the lighter load is significantly more pleasant. Although rarely used by Spaniards, 20- and 28-gauges are both no great disadvantage for this sport.

A partridge is an interesting target. According to various game bird speed charts, it has a maximum speed of about sixty-five miles an hour. A pheasant will approach seventy-five. (I have no idea if these numbers are accurate.) I have to admit that classic partridge beat me more often than tall pheasants do unless they are hugely high like the pheasants of Castle Hill. When caught by the wind, I find red legs a trickier target. When following the contours of the land, he is more deceptive. Deception and perception are closely linked, and its size has much to do with this. Once when shooting Rothwell as a guest of Lady Nicker-son, Joe's widow, I was killing my pheasants but missing some of my partridge, certainly more than I should have been. When I doubled what I thought was the correct lead, they started to hit the ground with regularity. I presume subconsciously I see a lead in terms of bird lengths. As David Nickerson, a nephew of the legendary Sir Joseph, points out, 'You get many different angles shooting partridge; much more variety than a pheasant straight overhead.'

I have for a long time been an advocate of tall pheasant shoots. It is nevertheless a mistake to try and make all birds fly in the same way. In Spain at the moment correct, proper, classic Spanish shooting is being frowned upon.

Ignacio Landaluce, who also owns a 'small' shoot in Spain – 100,000+ acres, about three hours south of Madrid – once said to me 'You are a well known tall bird shot. I will try and make things interesting for you in many ways; long crossers, undulating terrain, there are many ways to make partridge difficult and challenging, not just getting them high', echoing the view of Fernando.

The majority of foreign Guns choose not to go to the great estates and shoot the birds in their natural habitat, preferring to go to the ravined area near the towns of Chinchon or Toledo as they are very convenient to Madrid and the airport. Don't get me wrong, this is very good shooting and quite sporting, though one must choose operators carefully as some top up their birds as the season progresses and a few even release them from crates on the day. However, the demand is now so great for this type of shooting that many feel classic Spanish shooting is on the way out. That is absurd. It would be a tragedy. Fernando Bustamante, for a short time, also had the shooting at Layos, a good tall partridge shoot and ten minutes from Toledo. Nevertheless, he bemoans the emphasis on tall birds. 'Foreign Guns must understand that classic drives actually present the more difficult target: the bird that starts high, then drops and turns, that is a tricky target... You must explain that when you write, educate the foreign Guns, that is important.'

Layos used to be one of the great wild partridge shoots. It is particularly appealing as it is only about ten minutes from Toledo and quite close to Madrid. Because of the ravined nature of the territory, it showed tall partridge. Wild game such as partridge are subject to natural fluctuations in their population. This can be due to disease, an increase in predation, or a cold or wet snap before, during, or soon after hatching. Layos had these problems and the owner had to work very hard to rebuild his stock. Proud of his work and having rested his estate for a number of years, he invited a team of VIPs, all cognoscenti of partridge shooting in Spain, to his estate. Whether this is apocryphal or not I am not sure, but according to a friend, this is a true story: at the end of the day the bag was good, large by standards of any other country with roughly 800 wild partridge in the bag, but not up to expectations. 'Don't feel too badly, next time we'll do better,' a royal supposedly said. So upset was the owner that he rented out the land and it is now a good, but reared partridge operation.

Now there was one problem that I did not envision. This was a very mild year and shooting this late in the season, the male partridge were starting to fight for territory and breeding rights. Many of the red leg partridge, therefore, instead of flying where the beating team wanted them to go, flew back to the territory that they were protecting. Fernando did triumph over the perdiz and the bag was made or exceeded every day. But this did come at a cost. Because the line was so large and the birds so tricky to drive, one or two Guns were out of it on many drives. With twenty drives or so over three days it should even out statistically, but that's not always the case. Should I repeat this trip this late in the season again, I would limit the line to a maximum of eight, which is in general better anyway. (In this province the season runs from 8 October to 8 March.)

Much of what I know about driven partridge shooting, especially Spanish nomenclature, was covered in the Pinos Altos section and I will not revisit most of it. However, for many who have shot birds in the British Isles, Spain has some significant differences. The two most important are *pantallas*, metal plates placed on stakes at the side of the butt. They are designed to prevent the gun from swinging through the line and shooting a neighbour, similar in this way to stakes in the grouse butt. They're made of rectangular metal, which also prevents the odd errant pellet from hitting the shooter.

Occasionally, a small round *pantalla* is placed in front of the blind to block out the sun, a truly brilliant idea. (I have an ancient pair of shooting glasses that I bought in Spain about thirty years ago with metal sides to prevent an errant pellet from taking an eye. Today the same effect can be had much more comfortably with wraparound plastic safety lenses.)

The other item to revisit is the loader or *cargador*. The best loaders in Spain are the quickest that I have seen anywhere. They sit, back to the blind, in front and to the right of the shooter. On the bench attached to the front of their seats is a loading tray with cartridges placed rim up. One shoots, handing the gun forward with your right hand while simultaneously the fore end of your second gun is slapped into the palm of your left hand. To be quick and efficient one should always be looking forward, waiting for the bird. This is true whenever one uses a stuffer or loader.

Interestingly, Las Golondrinas, Pinos Altos and La Nava – all traditional shoots of the first order – use this classic Spanish method of exchanging guns. Some of the Chinchon and Madrid shoots that cater to English and American sportsmen employ the English system of loading. La Cuesta offers a choice.

Fernando saved the best drive for last. This was a drive that had everything. The beaters started miles off, or so it seemed; many on horseback, which were used to break up the *barras* of partridge. We were placed near a reservoir, our backs to a stream, a gently sloping hillside just in front of us. We waited and waited for birds to arrive. The wind howled. Some birds, flying into the wind, appeared to do nothing, but would drift from side to side making the line very difficult to read. Often, they would turn ever so slightly, catch the wind and be past the butt in the blink of an eye. Some birds were forty, fifty or even more yards high. Others were at eye level or below. But all were interesting, always challenging, and a joy to behold. *We killed 630 birds on the drive.* This was late February. Suddenly we were into overage, except that Fernando, the great sportsman that he is, decided not to charge it.

At the end of the drive, he came over to me and asked me what I thought. I was speechless. Fernando said, 'I wanted you to see what I can still do this late in the year.'

La Cuesta – The World's Best Tall Partridge Shoot

Every year, when I am not shooting sky-high pheasant in the British Isles, I lead a few teams to Spain to shoot the magnificent red-legged partridge. This year my December group had three Guns cancel at the last minute. I was 'up the creek without a paddle', as the saying goes, at about nine grand a man for three big days of sport. Having never met the owner, I was embarrassed to say the least. Tail between my legs, I called the owner Jesus Alberto Muela. 'Not to worry,' he said. 'We will just reduce the bag accordingly.'

I have written on both sides of the Atlantic about partridge shooting. I have shot some of the great classic estates like Rothwell in Lincolnshire where Sir Joseph Nickerson and his team shot the modern record bag of 2,000-plus birds. Most of these were wild greys, lovely birds whose numbers have been greatly depleted – not by over shooting but by loss of habitat and a concurrent change of farming practices. And I have shot in Spain at Las Golondrinas, perhaps my favourite classic shoot, where my own team once shot 637 fabulous birds on a single drive.

Yet nothing prepared me for the staggering quality of partridge – perdiz in local lingo – at the La Cuesta shoot.

Jesus Alberto Muela is a serious man, as the Spanish would say. 'I try to be a very proper man,' he told me. 'I try to do everything in the correct and proper way,' he said in his clipped English.

'I try to be as well,' I said. 'We may have a misunderstanding someday,' I continued, 'but it will only be, I believe, because we do not truly share a common language.'

They have two first-rate lodges called *fincas*. Las Beatas is a more traditional Spanish house. Set high on a hillside, La Cuesta is more modern with absolutely stunning views of the surrounding countryside. Its real advantage is that one is in the centre of the property for the day's shoot. (In total, they control over 100,000 acres; the La Cuesta part of the property, which produces the tallest birds, is about 20,000 acres.)

This is La Mancha. Las Beatas is situated close to the town of Villahermosa. The shoot is owned and run by Jesus Muela and his amazingly hardworking son Jesus Alberto – the Jesus referred to throughout. Using the available terrain, excellent partridges are shown off ground, which varies from undulating olive groves (traditional drives) to steep-sided hills. These hills often change to cliffs and, therefore, show the best tall partridge in Spain.

Muela employs about twenty full-time keepers. They organize in excess of 100 shooting days with typical bags ranging from 400 to 800 birds, although bigger bags can be had. The season runs from 8 October until 8 February.

Our team gathered at the lodge on Tuesday 9 December. We had come, almost literally, from the ends of the earth. Jim Egan is an Irishman living in England who has worked hard and now plays hard. He shoots with the enthusiasm and dedication that he must have put into the building of his companies. His driven shoot schedule, ninety-one days this season, is staggering. It starts with grouse and ends with five back-to-back days of Spanish partridge in the Salamanca region. (One must be careful picking shoots in Spain, especially so in Salamanca, as a very popular shoot there, represented by agents who should know better, releases birds from crates on each drive!)

Our betrothed friends Frank Sekula and Kendall Cook, now married, both living in England although they are American, joined us along with a client of Frank's, Richard Barnes. Henrique Menezes from Portugal, whom I met last season, proved a great addition to the line. Edwin Rodriguez, Rod to his friends, is a banker from Louisiana who shoots very well indeed with a lovely pair of classic Lang shotguns. And last, my email pen pal Serge Dompierre who shoots almost exclusively with a small bore 28-gauge Perazzi on a true 28-gauge frame. Serge owned and ran the best dove operation in Cordoba, meaning the best dove shooting the world, which now belongs to David Perez who has done much to improve it. Dompierre kept his eye in by shooting two to three days a week at the tallest of dove. He shoots his guns choked extra full with lethal elegance and effectiveness.

Introductions were made, a fine meal enjoyed and then we went off to sleep. The plan was simple enough: awake at 8, breakfast at 8:30, then depart for the shoot at 9:15.

A ride of a little over half an hour brought us to our first drive of the day at the base of a small cliff face. The birds were tall enough to be challenging but not intimidating. It is always a good idea on the first drive of the shoot or even of the day to let the team get their eyes in. The second drive provided a few more birds than the first and slightly taller. One thing was obvious, four of the six shots were absolutely first-rate, one was good and Frank's client, new both to partridge and to double gunning, was struggling a bit. Still, it is rare to have such a strong team. Normally in a line of eight, one has one or two fine shots, four average and two weak.

I spoke to Jesus, 'Can we pump this up a bit?'

'I've been holding back to keep to the contracted number of birds with the smaller line.'

'I'll speak to the team, but I have shot with most of them before and I think overage – *paying for extra bird shot* – should not be a problem. Just keep quality high as well.'

A quick conversation with the group confirmed my suspicions. 'Keep the birds coming, we are here to shoot,' said Jim, a sentiment echoed by all.

'No bag limit,' I said to Jesus.

'Are you sure?'

'I'm sure.'

Jesus asked my better half in Spanish to confirm what he thought he heard me say. 'Very well,' he said, and with this he pulled out all the stops. Things became truly interesting, hot-barrel action.

For a variety of reasons I was sharing a peg with Henrique who was just getting used to his brand-new pair of Arrizabalagas, which are from, along with Garbi, probably Spain's finest gunmaker. He was, indeed, being tested by the birds presented.

Whether the advice was wanted or not, 'Take them earlier,' I chimed in. 'Don't wait for the birds to be on top of you, shoot the first barrel.' (My incarnation as a shooting instructor reared its ugly head.) But the advice worked and his confidence grew and he had magnificent shooting of which he fully took advantage.

My turn again. I shot the first drive with a borrowed pair of Spanish guns. This drive, I shot with a gun borrowed from Jim, a Browning B2G. The gun fit and shot well, but a single gun is not enough. For this type of shooting, a pair of guns is necessary. (The reason I was shooting borrowed guns is that my pair that I was bringing for this shoot, useless things made by Famars – aka A&S, aka

Abbiatico and Salvinelli – had broken down after just being overhauled during the first drive shooting in England the day before I left for Spain.)

I was shooting the odd number drives and my pal the even. On drive number four, Henrique was in a brilliant spot as were Jim and Serge. His form locked on, he shot fifty-seven partridge, none less than thirty-five yards high and most taller, many much taller. At the end of the drive all the shooters were grinning from ear to ear.

In England one often encounters sewelling. Sewelling is colourful material strung on long stretches of rope. When pheasant, being pushed by a beating line, approach this mock fence, a designated man tugs on the line, shaking it to cause the birds to rise more vertically at the flushing point. This in turn presents taller, ergo, more testing, birds. Jesus Alberto has taken it one step further by putting out miles of fencing to accomplish the same thing. Fences called *berja* are laced with green metal plates called *chape verde*. Perdiz flying towards the fence are forced to climb for the heavens. Whereas sewelling is inexpensive, this is not.

Next it was my turn.

My peg was the Cruz part of the drive. We had to cross a small stream at the base of the ravine to take the birds coming back over us. Shooting the Browning with the selector set for the top barrel allowed me to reload more quickly if only one shot was taken. One loads double guns and one stuffs single guns. So I was using a stuffer. Loaders are called *cargadors* in Spanish. *Secretarios* count the birds killed with a clicker and mark where they fall. Both carry all the shooter's gear. By using clickers, shooters can be charged accurately and fairly for overage.

The birds on this side of the drive seemed to curl less than on the Cara but were even taller and faster if that were possible. I killed thirty superb birds with about two boxes of shells. Even choked modified (half) and improved modified (¾) these tall partridge hit with the first barrel sometimes required a second shot to dispatch. It was an awesome drive.

It was Henrique's turn for the last drive of the day. He was exhausted from his previous go and declined. I, too, felt I had shot enough so I let my better half, Renata, take my place. It took her a while to get her eye in with the borrowed Browning, especially as it was too long for her, but eventually the timing came, and with my incessant coaching she did add eight birds to the bag.

The final bag for the day, in this area called Montizon, was over 800 birds. Still, it was not easily accomplished. According to Jesus Alberto the better teams average about five cartridges to one bird on the tall drives, a typical team seven to one and some struggle at ten to one. Yikes. Luckily, we were a strong team with the four best shooters averaging under three for one.

After the shoot everyone commented on the unbelievable quality of the birds. Amazingly, the next day proved even better.

It was a forty-minute drive from Las Beatas to La Cuesta where we would shoot the next day. Perched on top of the hill, surrounded by more hills and valleys and ravines, this twelve-year-old house is the ultimate partridge destination. Unfortunately, it was already booked for the dates that suited our group. La Cuesta with sixty-six drives on its 20,000 acres can actually have two shooting parties going on at once, groups never meeting.

It was Henrique's turn to shoot first this day so I took my camera and headed off to stand behind Richard. Although from England, Richard had never shot double guns before. This was proving a challenge for him. I showed him how it was done, and pushed him to challenge his target by shooting it in front, giving time for a second shot *before* the partridge was directly overhead. He improved dramatically.

In classic, traditional partridge shooting, one's loader sits in front of the Shot and hands the gun up to the shooter. It is very quick, much quicker indeed than the traditional English style. However, for safety's sake many commercial shoots in Spain train their loaders to shoot the English way. This shoot is one of them. (Actually, they will load either style now.)

The birds on this drive were sky-high. Most were over forty yards up and although few were out of shot, many were definitely at the limits. Serge Dompierre was being pushed past the limit or at least past the limit of a 28-gauge gun.

'In all my years of shooting tall pheasant, duck and dove, I have never felt so under-gunned,' he said. His guns are choked extra full and extra full – Perazzi number ten chokes. However, the 28-gauge guns just did not have enough density in the pattern to consistently take down super-tall birds. Some birds did exceed the limit of any gun choke and cartridge combination and one just had to smile and admire them as they flew past. They were being driven off tall hills nearly half a mile away.

My turn on the second drive again proved an immense challenge. Finally, Henrique offered me his pair of guns. I quickly and gratefully accepted. These were the fourth set of guns I had used in the last three shoot days and it took a bit of time to get a feel for them. All guns have a different dynamic, depending on their weight and their point of balance. The fit, however, was pretty close, though I normally shoot with a bit more castoff. Off to one side and slightly out of the drive, I still managed to down twenty fantastically tall partridge.

If one shoots in Spain, with a Spanish team, one will soon learn that a

Spaniard prefers shooting his neighbour's bird to his own. They are competitive to the extreme and find it quite amusing. Shooting in England, it is very frowned upon to shoot one's neighbour's birds. It is important with a mixed team to set out guidelines. In general, I feel the English system is more equitable. However, if there are a hundred birds in the air at one time it really doesn't matter much. But even in this situation, one should not shoot the birds directly over the neighbouring gun, instead taking the birds closest to one's own peg.

Following this drive, we then drove to a different part of the estate where the new road was not yet completed. (Now finished, it looks like a super highway.) A driver approached a soft streambed with insufficient momentum, then accelerated madly and too late, firmly imbedding the Land Rover in the muck. Jesus was even a pro at handling these situations and quickly towing alternatively both from front and back, quickly had us on our way again. The weather was fabulous, bright sunshine and warm, very un-English, so all the Guns sat on a hillside to view the event. Had Jesus not been so quick, we probably could have enjoyed a siesta.

Another lovely drive followed and all the Guns were now getting truly into form. While we normally would have broken at this point for lunch, instead we put the fourth drive-in first so that Frank and his client could catch a late flight back to London as they had early meetings the next day. (It is much better to skip lunch than a drive.) Lunch and dinner were sumptuous repasts matched with excellent Spanish wines. We parked the cars near an old farmhouse from which we could view the snow-capped Andalusia mountain range. We walked along a road that followed a stream that sat beneath a cliff sixty yards high. It formed a loose L and that is how the Guns were placed.

'V de B' was the mother of all drives. Birds came out by the dozen and by the hundred; curling, curving and flapping their wings at the last minute to turn left when a nanosecond before the line was to the right. A strong wind at the cliff face turned this into the ultimate challenge. These partridge were so high that feathers would show up yards below where they had been hit, and they would fly on for another second or two before suddenly dying. *If the pellets did not kill them, the fall surely did.* Somehow I managed to pull forty-one birds from the heavens. The shooting was just too good to be believed and, my arms shaking, I turned the guns over to Henrique to finish the drive. He shot another thirty-seven birds.

We were, as it turned out, the amateurs. Jim Egan was in the zone. He shot 146 birds. This drive was the single greatest display of presenting birds that I can recall in over twenty-five years of shooting Spain. (Subsequently, I have seen this partridge drive surpassed twenty or thirty times but always and only at La Cuesta.) Never have I seen birds that were the equal. Jesus Alberto's sister, Maria, is also involved in the operation. She told me that they have a number of drives as good or better than this including Cara Y Cruz de la Communista, Los Caballos, La Nave, La Cruz de la Nave, and my favourite name, El Risko, which is so hard she said that it is for professionals only! The total for the day was over 900 perdiz.

The third day I awoke with a cold. I rolled back in bed, ordered room service and told them to wake me up in time for the third drive. (Typically, one shoots four to six drives in a day.) The extra sleep helped a lot. (Also, I was well into overage.) I drove to the shooting grounds on a different part of the huge area that they control. This was flat classic partridge terrain. The fields were dotted with chozo. I photographed during the drive, which provided a nice mix of classic with a few tall partridge that flew for the heavens not because they were coming off a cliff face but simply because they chose to sit on their tails and turn on the afterburners. The bag for the day was just over 100 partridge per man.

I can honestly say that this is the best tall partridge shoot in the world. Strangely, it is not the best classic partridge shoot. There are at least three or four that I would rate higher. And while I love a traditional shoot, I do so because I try and shoot it like a Spaniard, killing birds as quickly as possible, the first two way in front like grouse. Killing three or four birds out of a covey or flush is not easy – taking a single bird is. However, this is not the sensibility of all groups.

While Jesus and I will never speak the same language with the same degree of exactitude, we do understand each other well enough now to know what the other requires.

Since I wrote this for *Sports Afield*, I have shot La Cuesta four to nine days a year for seven more seasons. It gets better and better through a programme of improving drives and roads, creating more drives over newly acquired land. It is still the best tall partridge shoot I know.

La Flamenca and the Related Shoots

If there is a better-run shoot than La Flamenca, I do not know it.
I first heard of it from my good friend Pepe Fanjul who has been shooting
there for years. Pepe praised it highly and he should know as he has been
shooting in the UK – the Duke of Northumberland's, Wemmergill, Biddick,
Gunnerside, Prescombe, Rothwell and other top estates – for decades.

In addition to running seamlessly from the time one has been picked up at
the airport, the five shoots near Madrid of the Corsini family are also cheesy
with partridge. (They also organize true wild bird shoots near Jerez/Cadiz
through a consortium of farmers. These wild bird shoots all take place during
the first month of the season after which time raising bulls and farming takes
precedence for the owners. Javier Corsini was in a unique position to put this
together as he has his own *finca* in the area where he raises fighting bulls.) I
shot La Flamenca twice last year, finishing my season in early March. Shooting
with a team of Spaniards, we bagged 1,250 birds. Now I know that this sort of
big bag is frowned upon by many; the birds being a mix of tall drives and
traditional drives provided superlative sport. And while it was a bit over the
top, indeed my biggest day in years, I must admit I enjoyed every moment of
it. The point that I'm making is that one must have a lot of birds on the ground
to be able to accomplish the feat with just a week left to the end of season. These
birds are free ranging, properly driven perdiz, not the birds coming out of
crates.

The shooting is also exceptional value when compared with Great
Britain. When one considers that this includes airport transfers, hotel transfers,
cartridges, breakfast, lunch, licences and insurance, it is really tough to beat.
Nevertheless, with 500 birds as minimum, it is not an inexpensive shoot, although
costs can be ameliorated by shooting a team of nine or ten.

One is greeted at the airport by a driver who speaks good English and takes care of gun clearance. If you are coming from the UK all you need is your Euro pass. A maximum of three guns may be brought at any time by foreign sportsmen. Non Euro pass holders will need to get a licence from their Spanish Consulate. The driver then takes you to your choice of hotel or lodge. One can stay at the Ritz or other hotels in Madrid and without traffic make it to the various shoots in half an hour to forty-five minutes. Or one can stay at Paradors in Chinchon or Toledo, a hotel in Aranjuez, or stay at their lodge with nine bedrooms at their shoot called Fuensauco. The lodge makes most sense for teams who want to be on their own and who are primarily shooting Fuensauco or Casa Sola. This brings the price up slightly.

In the last two years, I have shot four of their five estates, all save Tacones. Each property has a dedicated room in a lodge or a purposely renovated building for breakfast and lunch. Both meals are outstanding as are the tapas and tacos provided between drives. The wines, too, are first rate, normally a good vintage Rioja. A magnum of CUNE Imperial is on the table at breakfast, although I do not recall it being consumed. Good cigars, Montecristo and the like, are also provided. The bathrooms, separate facilities for men and women, are also well decked out with grooming essentials. While in a way this is irrelevant to shooting, it shows an attention to detail that is rarely seen elsewhere.

La Flamenca, owned by the Duke of Nunez, was Javier Corsini's first shoot, which he has now been running for over twenty years. There are forty-two drives on a vastly diverse topography. While most Spaniards prefer traditional drives, there are also tall and very tall drives, especially in an area called 'The Speelman Valley' named after one of Javier's best friends. This is also undoubtedly one of the great classic partridge shoots of Spain. The birds come over the hills and offer many angles especially those perdiz that turn left or right with the terrain, offering tricky angles for birds thirty to forty yards in front. An exit from the new highway from Madrid virtually at the front gate makes it an easy commute. Leaving wild bird shoots aside, this is perhaps the King's favourite shoot, as some years he is here twenty days.

Casa Sola is just a few minutes from the town of Chinchon. The town square is actually oval as it is a bullfighting venue. (Interestingly, there are no cases of bullfighting hooliganism – footballers take note.) The Parador is very good and there are nice restaurants in the town – great suckling pig and other local specialities are worth savouring. The shoot itself offers very challenging birds. In the first area we shot they proved too tough for two members of our team so we went to a different area within the estate that still provided difficult birds, some not so tall were mixed in so as not to discourage or dishearten these Guns. Some really outstanding drives for discerning tall bird Shots are available.

Fuensauco on the other side of Chinchon offers undulating terrain and cliff faces and provides perhaps the tallest drives of the five shoots. The lodge is one of the nicest I've visited anywhere in Spain and the dining room, filled with trophies from Spain and Africa, is very appealing. The food was delicious. One member of the team, Majid Jafar, was staying at the Ritz and made it down on Saturday morning in twenty-five minutes.

Casa de los Conejos is very similar terrain to Fuensauco and quite close to La Flamenca. I believe the literal translation is 'house of the rabbit'. I shot it once last year and once this year and both times it was excellent.

Tacones is the furthest from Madrid but still only sixty miles and on the far side of Toledo. I have not shot it but its *Cara y Cruz*, also known as reverse drives, are said to be among the best in Spain.

Javier Corsini is an elegant gentleman of the first order. Charming and sophisticated, a subtle wit shows just how good his English is. At the age of six, his father would take him rabbit hunting with a single-barrel 9-mm rifle. By the age of twelve, he was shooting stag in Monterias. Working with an English friend, James Stewart, who lived in the south of Spain, they started shooting wild partridge commercially nearly thirty years ago. Twenty years ago, or there-abouts, they started to shoot La Flamenca commercially. As time went on, more shoots came under their control, including one near Seville called Fuente Luenga, which they still run. Javier Corsini has always made it a point of working with friends. His brother Eduardo joined the company about twelve years ago and today Eduardo's son, also named Eduardo, also runs shoots. The last member of their team is Ignacio de Navasques, a fine young man whose English is excellent and who ran the three days for our shoots last November. (He is well educated with degrees in economics and is the son of one of Javier Corsini friends.)

Our team was eclectic and included my friend Majid Jafar, who if I were redoing my 'Dream Team' would definitely make the cut. The other members of the team were John and Martha Johnson from America; John Hardy from England; two New Zealanders – Gary Gwynne and Martyn Coe; Laura Revitz, an American who spends a lot of time in Spain shooting live pigeon competitions; and myself. In our three days of shooting, each drive was unique, posing different problems to the shooters. Most of the drives were tall, some were very tall; but I did ask for some classic birds so that the two guns who were struggling on high, fast partridge could get their eye in. All the drives produced fast-flying, strong partridge. To describe the drives in detail would require much more space than I am allocated so let me just say that this is one of the two best shoots I know in Spain for the quality of shooting and the best run commercial operation that I know anywhere.

Part II – Great Britain and Ireland

Castle Hill – Castle Great

'It is a very grown up shoot,' said Keith Halsey to me regarding our planned day shooting with the syndicate at Castle Hill. He was right. He was right in spades, but I get ahead of myself.

For quite a while three shoots have eclipsed the rest of the West Country in their notoriety for being truly great, the other two being North Molton and Haddeo. Reputation is a funny thing. Gun fighters in the old west often did not have to get into fights simply because most were scared to take them on while others, such as the legendary Wild Bill Hickok, were shot in the back by some punk trying to make a name for himself. Shoots are a little bit like that. People have often heard so much about a shoot with a reputation that they are slightly intimidated on arrival and sometimes think they are getting better shooting than in fact they are. On the other hand even the best shoots will have an off day due in part, most commonly, to weather conditions that were unforeseen.

Because I have been around as much as I have, I often go to a shoot expecting a bit less than its reputation, and I am pleasantly surprised if it comes close. For example, Chargot, which is undoubtedly one of the best known of the West Country shoots and is normally rated with four stars by the magazines that do such articles, was worth three and a half stars on the day that I shot there. To be fair weather conditions were against them; but to be critical they put too many medium birds into what is colloquially referred to as 'bag-fillers' or 'killing' drive for the first. Molland and West Molland, which I shot four times last season and which receives five stars from the same magazines, was worth perhaps four on the days I shot in November and four and a quarter in December, and they gave me all their best drives. (To receive five stars for shooting on the Brant scale, extreme and deceptive birds must be in the mix.) I am not referring to birds at or beyond the limit of range. These are archangels, tall pheasant, which are not too high to kill, but rather at or near the limit of range; and with enough speed, curl or slip to beat most good Guns most of the time. Even at West Molland Wood, perhaps the best of that shoot's drives, in the two days that I saw it, only had one archangel in it, which I luckily did manage to bring down. One extreme bird does not an extreme drive or extreme day make. Also, the birds at Molland and West tended to be straightforward with relatively little curl or drift on them. In other words they were, perhaps, too killable. This brings me back to Castle Hill. Most of the birds on most of the drives, while being killable were very challenging if one went for the lower birds, and awesomely challenging in the extreme, perhaps even intimidating, if one chose the taller pheasants. That said, I saw many pheasant at the limit of range, but none out of range. No wonder some refer to Brian Mitchell, the headkeeper, as 'god'.

The night before the shoot the group convened at Northcote Manor Hotel. I had travelled down from Inverness and had a taxi pick me up at Bristol airport. It was a very sensible thing to do as all the driving on the back roads can be quite tricky unless there is a navigator on board, the roads are known, or where GPS is working. It also made a lot of sense as we left directly after the shoot and I was so tired from shooting that I was dozing off as the passenger. While dozing off as a passenger can be pleasant, dozing off as the driver is not recommended.

The group that convened was extremely convivial. My room was next to Keith's and we had a quick chat when he arrived. He had driven down from a friend's family shoot in the Cotswolds and he was tired when he arrived. As he knew everyone, and I knew no one, we decided to go down to dinner together. First to arrive was Caspar MacDonald-Hall, the captain of the syndicate, who is widely acknowledged as being one of the best all round shots in Britain. A very urbane and sophisticated gent, he gets so much great shooting, sixteen days on grouse, that if he weren't so likeable, one would feel envious.

The Drives on the Day

Drive 1 – Tilleries

While my peg number seven, last on the left, was probably the slowest and easiest peg, even the birds at my end had nice slip and curl to them and were not 'give me' sort of birds. It also afforded me the opportunity to watch the team shoot. The birds at the lower pegs were excellent and the Guns up to it. (We were shooting a line of seven.)

Drive 2 – Deer Park

Deer Park is a picturesque drive with a stream behind the Guns. What an amazing, though slightly intimidating, drive. Wave after wave of unrelenting, tall birds were presented. Again, I was on the slow end but still shot over seventy cartridges. Keith, two pegs to my left, and shooting a single gun, fired 170. I've seen birds taller but rarely faster. I left as many birds as possible on my right for George Goulandris, a good sporting man, fine shot and member of the syndicate, who was a bit out of it. After the drive ended, Keith aka 'The Tosh' told me that with the deluge of birds over the Gun to my left, 'it is not necessary to be so circumspect'.

Drive 3 – Hobbs Wood

Not normally considered a signature drive, it was, from my peg in any case, the drive of the day; perhaps a drive of a lifetime. I was on peg four, normally the best peg. The wind was so strong from right to left that the higher pegs, sometimes a bit out of it, had lots of shooting for birds this day, that had they been any faster, would have set off missile defence systems.

It was the physically most intimidating drive that I have ever viewed. Birds were being launched across a long, steep hillside hundreds of yards distant and with a line of tall trees acting as super-sewelling. I killed more amazing pheasant than on any drive in donkeys' years. Some were so good that I stopped shooting for the few seconds of their fall – seemed like half an hour – just to enjoy the shot. The strong wind from right to left (easterly) forced birds to come with extreme speed and curl.

Drive 4 – Brayley

Another signature drive, this one, too, is physically beautiful as it is located near the old railway bridge, which is a monument in stone and testament to Victorian engineering. Beautiful masonry piles now form an aqueduct. I killed birds both coming over and going right to left along the line of woods in front. The big flush of incredible birds towards the end of the drive actually proved physically and mentally exhausting. Not as difficult as the previous two but still a five-star drive anywhere.

Drive 5 – Smoldon's Bottom

I was supposed to be peg one and since we were shooting a team of seven, I was moved to peg eight as the lower pegs are not as good here. The beating team drove the wood above, but lost a lot of birds early to the left of the line because a stag, of all things, ran through the drive. He was undoubtedly disturbed by the beaters and it was a most unusual occurrence. Brian had me scurry up the bank to try and cut off the errant birds flying that way, and killed between twenty and thirty birds, including a couple of doubles and a few times three or four birds in a row as one-barrel kills. A great end to one of my best days ever.

Brian Mitchell has been at Castle Hill for twenty seasons. He has four beatkeepers and generally has twelve pickers-up on the day. With thirty-two drives to choose from, it gives him a great advantage to be able to choose drives on the day based on weather conditions and the quality of the team. His signature drives include Deer Park, Brayley, Proutworthy, Smoldon's Bottom, Eggersford Bank, May's Quarry, Punch Bowl and Collythorne.

There is probably no more important gamekeeper in the history of the West Country than Brian Mitchell. With the owner Alan Milton, he turned Miltons from a small syndicate shoot into the first of the great West Country tall bird shoots. He also created Bulland and significantly improved Chargot by opening up more ground, by getting the opposite valleys leases and so forth. He hired Nick Boniface, who is still there, to be the headkeeper there when he left. If this were not enough, he also set up the Challacombe partridge shoot for the first four years, where John Brooks is now the headkeeper. Mitchell's son, Robert, is the brilliant headkeeper at North Molton.

Brian speaks of what he calls a golden barometer:

Whether it is air pressure or thermals, I do not know. It only happens about twice a year and it does not last long, perhaps half an hour. But when it does occur, the birds fly out of their skin. On a similar day, without this golden barometer, the birds could not be bothered. It doesn't matter if it is windy or still, something just happens to make them sit on their tail and want to fly. You see the same effect on decoying pigeons or in a different version even out lamping fox.

Castle Hill and North Molton are so special because they have such a variety of drives. It is no good picking drives for a given day a week ahead. Conditions could be all wrong. I choose the drive on the day depending on the wind direction and other factors.

The more birds I can get missed, the happier I am. I do not mean that I put birds out of range. That is not fair. Rather, I present birds with a lot of drift and at different speeds. On some drives with a strong south-westerly wind and a dip in the terrain, show pheasants that are slipping a lot and many Guns don't read them right. It is a little like a cat playing with a mouse. I try and read the body language of the Guns when they are shooting. Even if they say they are happy, their body language will tell me if they are truly struggling and are downhearted. If they are struggling I often switch to easier drives. I don't want to over-face Guns or teams.

At lunch, 'The Great Day' was discussed. 'The Great Day' raised a lot of money for charity last season. As Haddeo is closing down, this charity shoot, where one great drive was offered at each of the four top West Country shoots, various suggestions were being bandied about as to a shoot to replace it. Someone suggested West Molland Wood, which I said it wasn't good enough. Another asked what I meant by that and I responded I could kill all the birds there. At this Brian suggested I was an honest man.

Castle Hill is owned by the Fortescue family and the great house is available to rent for various venues and this can be found by Googling. It was a great pleasure to watch Lady Margaret picking up.

North Molton

I first learned of North Molton about a decade ago from an acquaintance from the Racquet & Tennis Club, Nick Barham. Nick, a Brit who lived in America for a time, was a very highly ranked hard racquets player who in fact, if memory serves, won the US national championship, he certainly won the Racquet & Tennis Club championship; and because he is such a fine athlete, with excellent hand–eye skills, has often made the top fifty shots of England list in a number of magazines. Nick was one of the main members of the North Molton syndicate and often offered me double days for my own teams. Unfortunately, indeed regrettably, he did so back in the days when we were running our shoots at Humewood and Shillelagh and I could never commit early enough to procure the days.

I finally made it to North Molton five or six years ago with a group put together by my friend Frank Sekula, a successful American-born, London-based banker. Frank, much to his credit, got seriously into shooting after his move to England. He did a great job of finding similarly minded friends, some of whom he converted to our sport.

I have been to a number of great shoots prior to this, but nothing quite on the same scale. North Molton shoots many days each week, starting with partridge in September and switching to pheasant as the season progresses. Robert Mitchell is the brilliant headkeeper who runs the day from start to finish, acting as both headkeeper and shoot manager on the day. Everything at North Molton is done simply, but beautifully.

On arrival in a converted farm building, one is greeted with coffee and assigned loaders, and there are excellent cartridges available if necessary. But it is not until one is pegged on the first drive and the birds start to fly that the seriousness and the quality of the shoot becomes apparent.

Robert is one of the two most astute gamekeepers that I have come across in the West Country, the other being his father, Brian, at Castle Hill. Like Brian he works at testing the Guns by presenting birds that are exceptionally deceptive. On this day they were *too* deceptive. The wind was huge, if not a gale then close, and with the addition of all the curl, these were the most difficult birds that I ever had the pleasure of shooting (or more accurately shooting at). This was my first day of driven shooting that season, and I had just arrived back from New York, so I was slightly jetlagged. Also I had stupidly, and stupid is the only word for it, brought a light though well choked pair of side-by-sides. The cartridges, though excellent, were very fast and in my Perazzi's would have been a pleasure to shoot. But my light game guns, though capable of physically handling the cartridges, just beat me up. The fact that I fired nearly 500 cartridges on the day did not help. While I did not develop a flinch, it did put my timing off and this is all the prelude to the fact that I am looking for an excuse to explain why I shot so badly.

In truth, there are very few Shots who are truly capable of handling the big birds on the top drives at Castle Hill or North Molton. Anyone who shoots a bird for fewer than six cartridges is shooting well. Certainly there are great Shots who on their day will break the one-to-three ratio, though it would take a George Digweed or Peter Schwerdt to matter-of-factly accomplish this.

They start shooting in early September with very tall partridge and perhaps the two best partridge drives are Barrow Clifftops and Beeches. In October the days become mixed with pheasant added in and these early mixed days are largely partridge, which saves enough pheasants early on to produce consistently large pheasant bags right until the end of the season. Beeches is probably the best mixed drive. Both of them are top drives as well along with Larches, Leewood, Huntstown, Cowlane, Vennwood.

Rookery is an amazing drive where the birds are pulled a tremendous distance and then run the gauntlet of virtually the entire line. This is done with amazing style and great height and sometimes there are a thousand birds in the air. Robert Mitchell is, as a friend of mine who often shoots North Molton points out, 'a thinking man's keeper. If it's too warm and flat he will organize lunch early, so that the afternoon, with the temperature dropping, will provide better shooting.'

For example, early in the season he will shoot Barrow Clifftops early in the day, even though it shoots best at the very end of the day, so as not to push too many birds through. Later in the year he will shoot it as the last drive of the day. Also, because they have a lot of ground on which they shoot, he will shoot one drive in one area and then leave it completely, going to another drive a fair distance away, so that because of the large quiet area, birds are not overly disturbed.

Additionally, later in the year when there are insufficient birds in a game crop, he will plough in that cover crop to be able to then pull the birds into another drive, concentrating the number of pheasant.

Perhaps I am a masochist but I enjoy the shoots where I struggle to shoot well much more than the shoots where I always shoot well. If one is comfortable with really being tested as a Game Shot, pushed to the limits both in terms of one's own hand–eye coordination and the use of equipment suitable for the job (heavy guns, tight chokes and number 3 or 4 shot), then one can do no better than North Molton.

Prescombe

I first met Steve Thomas at Biddiscombe or Oakford, I can't remember which, back in the days when he had those shoots as well as Prescombe. His right-hand man, Nigel Brown, was sitting on my left at lunch and Steve on my right. The smallness of the world is eerie, as Nigel had contacted me a short time earlier about arranging some shooting for himself and friends in Argentina. Steve had opened one of the nicest bottles of red wine that I have encountered on a commercial day, which got us talking on that subject. Steve is renowned for both the good food and even better wine that he serves. The day had been exceptionally wet and had someone dropped a trout in my jacket pocket and had I not noticed it for eight hours, it would have lived. Nevertheless it was obvious that we had exceeded the bag even in those conditions. Steve in his good humoured and generous manner at the end of the shoot commented, 'Let me go see how many extra birds you shot that I am *not* going to charge you for.'

The following year I was speaking to my friend Jamie MacLeod and mentioned that I was flying down to shoot Cranbourne as the guest of our mutual friend Bruce Buck. Jamie said that he was hosting a shoot at Prescombe the following day and why didn't I stay the night between shoots with him and join his line.

I shot Cranbourne on the Friday with Bruce Buck, which was a most enjoyable day. The group had a convivial night before at the Museum Inn. Cranbourne was a single gun day, but because my old back cannot handle carrying guns and cartridges, they kindly organized a nearby keeper to stuff for me. At the end of the shoot, I drove cross-country, got slightly lost and used my cell phone to call Jamie MacLeod who talked me in, on the last half mile.

A large number of Jamie's friends made it down on Friday night for dinner before the shoot. The next morning found us at Prescombe. Jamie, being a great sportsman, had particular instructions for the shoot. He didn't care if we made the bag for which he paid as long as we failed to make it because the birds beat us. (I gave the same instructions to Drynachan but they ignored it, q.v.)

Steve Thomas and the headkeeper, Simon Hawker, did their best to oblige, presenting drives with exceedingly tall and testing red legs.

I doubt there was one bird killed in the entire day that was not sporting. The end of November was getting late in the partridge season and while there were not the huge number of birds to be expected in September/October there were still plenty of birds about to test our skills. While I shot very well the day before at Cranbourne, I was not up to snuff on this day. Five bad discs slow me down on days when I do have to carry my own gun and cartridges or perhaps the birds were just too fast or doing something I was not correctly reading. The birds were often driven in both directions as reverse drives but not all of our six drives were reverse drives. My good friend Pepe Fanjul often shoots Prescombe early when birds are abundant and Prescombe is one of his favourite British partridge shoots. Steve is capable of placing Guns on the day based on conditions and does so each day instead of pegging. It works very well.

'We do not have pegs, we place everybody. We feel it's important that, when we place Guns, it looks and feels that nobody else has been there before. It's also easier to cover the whole line by birds flying over Guns,' states Thomas.

Steve Thomas produced a wonderful day's sport with his usual terrific elevenses, lunch and wines. We shot through and had lunch at the end of the day. But we had intelligently organized a bus to bring us back into Southampton where the group had convened for breakfast in the morning so no one drove under the influence even though the lunch was exceedingly lengthy.

Steve and I renewed our acquaintanceship at lunch and being the kind and generous sportsman that he is, he invited me to come back on the last day of the season to shoot as his guest on the day when he primarily invites the individuals from whom he rents the farmland for the shoot. The total acreage of the shoot is about 3,400 acres, on which he has thirty-four drives, the signature drives being: Hamilton's and Revenge, Monty's and Mandry's.

Renata and I had spent the night before with a friend of hers who lives in Dorset about twenty minutes from the shoot. We made an early morning run from our friends at Georgian Manor to Prescombe. We were almost late, because coming in this atypical way cross-country we wound up on a very narrow road just slightly larger than a single lane when a gigantic lorry came from the other direction. Renata did an excellent job of backing up but it does take a while to go half a mile in reverse around curves. When we did arrive, on time but just barely, we were greeted by a very nice group of charming but unknown to us sportsmen. Even at the end of the season Steve was able to concentrate enough birds into the drives to produce challenging sport.

At the end of the day, he kindly invited me back to shoot on 1 September, which is the other day he keeps for friends. Obviously there would be many more birds to challenge the line on the first day than the last, so being no fool, I immediately accepted. Occasionally life wreaks havoc on the best sporting plans. Midway through the summer it was suddenly determined that 1 September was to be the closing date on the Irish property I had directorship responsibilities and I had to be there. With deep and profound regrets, but with no way out, I had to cancel. Steve being a true gent immediately invited me for the next year on opening day instead. A book deal ensued on big game hunting in Africa tentatively entitled *Confessions of a Safari Addict*, which once again placed me in the wrong country on 1 September.

I am a great believer in never cancelling a shoot because of either a better invite coming along or the mundane aspects of life. Even though these were business obligations that I could not control, I have always felt like a bad sport for cancelling and it is only because Steve Thomas is such a gent and so understanding that he has chosen to forgive me.

Haddeo

I shot Haddeo on perhaps their last double day ever, on 14 and 15 January. If this proves to be the case, while not a tragedy on the scale of say, the Vietnam War, it will still prove to be a shame.

I came to get these days, scarce as hens' teeth, in a very curious fashion. For the longest time, Haddeo was owned by Sir Ned Goschen. A few years ago he sold his part of the property to Peter Shalson. Peter and his wife Polly were to be shooting with me at one of my mixed days at La Cuesta. When I was speaking to him to get this organized, Peter mentioned that he had a late cancellation on days normally kept for a team in mid January. I leapt at the opportunity. It proved the right decision as I have never had a shoot fill so quickly. Four emails did it, as each of the gents to whom I first offered it accepted and two had friends who also wanted to join the line. This was obviously based on Haddeo's fantastic reputation.

Haddeo had for the longest time been one of the West Country's three great shoots. While it does not have as much land or as many drives as Castle Hill, it still has plenty and its best drives are fantastic.

Strangely, the first drive of the first day (Charlie's) and the last drive of the second day (General's) were the only that failed to impress. The first drive did not have many birds in it or at least not many that went over the line, and this I believe was at least in part due to the fact that the wind direction was wrong. Only about thirty birds were killed on the first drive and being in the 'hot spot', I got the bulk of the shooting, although in retrospect I wish I had been in the right place on the last drive of the day, which was by far best drive of the two days. Actually, this first drive made me quite nervous, if it augured for the rest. The Guns had paid serious money for the day. With the number of birds seen on the first drive, there was no way we would have come close to our expected bag. Luckily the drives increased and improved both in volume and in quality with each new drive on the day. And as a warm-up drive the first was certainly acceptable. While I had planned on reviewing each drive in detail, as it is now likely that the shoot will be closing, although it may at some point in the future change hands and reopen, that much verbiage is no longer justified. Without going into too great detail, it must be noted that the ground shot at Haddeo is not owned entirely by Shalson, just as it was not owned in its entirety by Goschen, but leased.

Unfortunately for Shalson, – at least as I have been told – the fellow who owns the majority of the contiguous land, which is absolutely necessary for operating the shoot, has refused to renew the lease. Whether or not somebody else takes this on at a future date will need to be seen. Hopefully this will occur as it is far too good a shoot to lose. It should be noted that Peter did not stint on any money or effort to make this work. The shoot lunch takes place in a building specifically designed for the purpose. Traditional-looking from the outside, it is extremely modern in its interior. CNN or Bloomberg are shown on a big flat panel monitor and there is good wireless reception. Indeed, and it quite annoyed me, we went twenty minutes out of our way for elevenses where there was cell phone reception. I was told by the headkeeper, Derek Holley, that it was organized in this fashion. The shoot was so dependent on city types coming and they often got twitchy if they could not reach their office late morning. Personally, I would like to see cell phones banned in the field, except in the confines of the individual offender's vehicle.

While a bit over the top, this lunch folly was nevertheless exceedingly comfortable and well designed, with large full bathrooms, comfortable seating areas, a roaring fire and red stag horn chandeliers. The food was delicious and the wine was an excellent Bordeaux of good vintage.

Because Haddeo does not control all of the land, indeed the pens and where one is pegged are on the shoot ground proper, much of the area used to drive the birds is on the neighbouring estate.

The last drive of the first day was the best drive of either day as previously noted. It was called Swinescleave. It took place in a long valley with many equally good drives to its left and right. I was back gunning behind my friend FM Claessens and Gary Troyer. This was both a pleasure and a misery. It was a pleasure because they both shot brilliantly and while I would not say that FM killed more birds than Gary, he certainly shot the equal and as he did so with a 28-gauge gun, he must be given the nod for the best shooting of the day. The misery was that I was behind both of them and on way too many occasions I would see a lovely bird coming to me, which was killed just as I began my mount. Still, I must have killed twenty or thirty excellent birds that each posed a very different problem. Birds going to my left were stalling due to the wind and those to my right were both accelerating and slipping away. It was because of their disparate speeds that it took me a while to hone in on them. Also most of them were at the limits of range to my left and right. (The birds over the frontline were actually taller as they had set their wings and were dropping for me.) I still managed to have a few left and rights, which was most gratifying. FM shot 170 cartridges on the drive.

The second day had an excellent first drive, one of the best of the season, with only Castle Hill's first drive being a better opener. The next two drives were excellent, with birds taller, the third being a new drive, supposedly never before shot. We were a team of seven and I was supposed to be on peg one but was moved to peg eight, as they felt that the shooting would be better there. Because it was a new drive to them and because of the strong wind going the wrong way, at least for me, I actually would have been better off on my original peg. Such are the vagaries of weather and the riskiness or vicissitudes of switching pegs. (Nevertheless, since a good gamekeeper will get this right much more often than wrong, I personally agree with the instinct to take this chance.) Indeed, I had the tallest birds over me on this drive and hit a hen that was so high that I will not say the yardage, because most people will not believe me.

The real shame and the sole shortcoming of the shoot is that they provided really crummy Rio cartridges – I would gladly have paid more for a premium load. On the previous day, on the best drive, I had to stop shooting to check my barrels, because I got one of those whooshing sounds, most often associated with homemade handloads. The first thing to do in this case is to check one's barrels to see if a wad is stuck. If it is, the barrels will either bulge or burst on the next shot – a rod must be used to clear them. The barrels were in fact clear. On examination of the cartridge the wad had turned sideways (fibre) and was still *inside* the cartridge. Had they provided the first-rate cartridges of nearby Castle Hill, the hen, which I hit hard six to eight inches too far back with the slower cartridge, would have been hit in the front third and fallen like a stone.

The last drive of the day showed the least tall birds of the shoot. We had had torrential rains during the night, though both shoot days were primarily dry, and I was told, although I am not certain, that the valley where we had the best shooting of the first day was not reachable. What a great pity to end on a drive that while full of birds was too much of a bag-filler.

That said, the best drives here were head and shoulders above even the best drives at West Molland or Chargot. Except for the first and last drive, the other six were all true five-star drives with tall, challenging and tricky birds, many at the limit of range.

The fellow acting as the host very kindly, and hopefully accurately, said that we were the strongest team of the season. Stealing a line from Hemingway at the end of *The Sun Also Rises*, 'It is pretty to think so.'

Stratfield Saye

I was spending a few days in London recovering from too much shooting and on my own while Renata went to Vienna for a funeral. I stayed at Brooks's on St James's during the week, but as the club basically closes down except for the bedrooms on the weekends, I decided to go around the corner and stay in a hotel for the weekend. It was the correct decision as the staff at Dukes was very gun friendly and the bar was both convivial and pro-cigar. On Saturday morning (yes there is an occasional Saturday that I don't shoot), I decided to make the round of stores working my way to Purdey's. I started my safari down Pall Mall at Farlow's where I ran into an acquaintance from Palm Beach, Bart Burnap, who had just come back from shooting some of the major West Country shoots. As we chatted, he asked me which was my favourite English shoot. Without thinking and not even sure why, I said the Duke of Wellington's Stratfield Saye Estate. (This was before I shot Castle Hill which would now get the nod.)

Now to be sure there are shoots in the West Country, in the north of England, in Wales and in Scotland that show taller birds. But at some point, it is not merely the height of the bird that determines the quality of a shoot. Stratfield Saye is one of my favourites for some very interesting reasons. First, it is the least commercial shoot (obviously excluding completely private) that I have ever been to. The family is sporting mad with most accomplished fly fishermen, stalkers, shooters and equestrians. This is true both of the men and the women. Indeed, the only days they let are the days when the family is occupied elsewhere. Being away pursuing sport is not surprising as the family own estates in Scotland and in Spain. Seventy to eighty per cent of the days are kept for the family and four to six days are let, a couple to locals and regular teams and the remainder discreetly through my Drivenshooting agency.

I first discovered this shoot through my friend and wonderful sporting gentleman, Richard Purdey. I asked him for a couple of recommendations for shoots near London and this was one of two. This is a shoot that he knows well as he has been taking a couple of days a season for himself and his guests for a number of years. Additionally, it is a unique opportunity for Guns to visit this amazing estate and to see it in such a close and intimate fashion. The Guns meet at the Museum, which is a fitting tribute to the Iron Duke. The Duke was given a sum of money after the Peninsular Wars and the Battle of Waterloo by Parliament to purchase an estate befitting his rank. The Museum shows the various stages of the Duke's career from soldier to politician and finally statesman, at all of which he excelled.

In a society as ours is now, where celebrity and fame are confused and both are mistaken for greatness it is often easy to forget the true greats of history, science or the arts. (There is something wrong when a hairdresser to a star makes more moolah than most university professors and when scoring goals at football creates more excitement than medical breakthroughs.) By all accounts, and even I am not old enough to have been there, the Iron Duke was a great man. There are some terrific quotes on the walls of the museum '…I hope to God that I have fought my last battle…I am wretched at the moment of victory, and I always say that next to a battle lost the greatest misery is a battle gained.' But I digress, back to the shoot.

Stuart Heath captained a team last November. We all met and stayed at Tylney Hall the night before where a terrific dinner was served in a private area making for a very suitable venue. It was a short drive from the hotel to the estate in the morning. The shoot team also included Raja Balasuriya, David Flux, Charles Heneage, Matthew Shuter, Rob Everett, Julian Avery and Henry Colthurst.

After viewing the Museum, fortified with additional caffeine, the pegs were drawn. We drove off and nowhere is it easier to get around, as the large estate boasts many paved roads. The birds on the first drive, the Duke's Cedar, were cracking. While height is much about the quality of pheasant shooting, it is not everything, and these birds were tall enough. But speed and deception are integral as well and these birds were exceptionally strong flyers with a wind that gave them both curl and slip. These birds had speed and deception in spades. Fifty-six pheasant and one red leg were bagged.

The team was quite strong, indeed better than most. One gent fairly new to shooting shot very well indeed, so well for his fifth driven day that I can only assume he had the intelligence to take some lessons. (I arranged a loader through

Paul Sedgwick, the resident agent, a chap named Andy Pye, who taught the Duke's grandchildren to shoot and it was obvious that Pye was coaching intelligently throughout the drives.) The spread of the birds was very good and while some pegs always get better shooting than others there was much activity.

Little Switzerland was named, I presume, with tongue in cheek as it is more of a hill than a mountain but with enough height and space to show tallish, testing birds. Abutting a lake, it is picturesque. Fifty-two pheasant and a foolish, lone pigeon were shot.

Elevenses were served on the front terrace of the house overlooking the main lawn and the Broadwater with champagne and King's Ginger and sloe being served, along with homemade roebuck sausages and other yummy items.

On to McKenzie clump where thirty-eight pheasant and one woodcock were added. This was followed by Tubbs where the majority of partridge, nineteen of twenty, were shot along with seventy-five testing pheasant. The next drive was lunch, the only one where I, too, was a participant.

There was one major flaw in the day – I wasn't shooting. It was bloody hard to watch such good birds and such a convivial group enjoying the fine sport without developing an itchy trigger finger. Previously, I took a day at Stratfield Saye to repay my own friends and it, too, was excellent. Interestingly, at the end of that day Paul Sedgwick, the most excellent resident agent, asked me what I would do differently. Without sounding too presumptuous, I did suggest a couple of things: a longer lunch period so that the Guns could have more time to tour the house with its special charms and unique historical features, and for a few minor changes at lunch, again designed to allow the Guns to linger, including port and cigars at the end of the meal. Lunch included the most delicious roebuck – I was told they hang it for ten days – accompanied by a '96 Chasse Spleen. (When the First Duke was in residence, and Queen Victoria visited, the Duke and Queen Victoria would dine at a small table in front of the window whilst the rest ate at the main dining table.) Portraits of the First Duke's family grace the walls.

The last two drives of the day were North End Pleasure Grounds and Parkside, which accounted for fifty and fifty-five pheasant respectively, and the latter the most diversity with two woodcock and one more pigeon. Then it was back to the museum for tea while the keepers and loaders cleaned the guns. Anyone who can get the opportunity to visit the Museum of the First Duke should.

In the end 351 birds were shot.

The First Duke was a keen sportsman but his life pre-dated the advent of breech-loading shotguns and the social heyday of the great shooting house parties. It was the second and third Dukes who established Stratfield Saye as a driven shooting estate. World War One saw the end of the grand Edwardian shooting tradition across Britain.

This did not mean that shooting ended but it did go though many phases, the most amusing, related in His Grace's article (*Shooting Gazette*, April 1998, page 30), was perhaps during his uncle the Fifth Duke's time, who had a particular preference…The Duke wrote:

> But above all he had a passion for rabbit shooting and all the big woods had rabbit rides cut in them at narrow points. Apart from these a large area of the park was turned into a rabbit warren covered in bracken, in which again large shooting rides were cut. The drill was the same before a shoot in both the woods and the warren. For a few days before the keepers would 'stink out' the rabbits, so that they were lying above ground. The woods or warren were then driven and hundreds of rabbits were shot crossing the rides. They were very difficult shots and some of the most sporting shooting I have ever done: You had to be extremely quick.

This shoot was run for a very long time by the Eighth Duke of Wellington. In 1968, after retiring from the Army, he began a studied approach to creating a shoot by planting trees, improving the quality of the pheasant stock, redesigning old coverts, adding game crops and all that is necessary to improve both habitat and sport. These are the acts of true conservationists and improved ecosystems for many species. (The term conservationist was coined by Gifford Pinchot, Teddy Roosevelt's Secretary of the Interior, both of whom were keen sportsmen – something of which modern urban tree huggers seem unaware.)

For a number of years now the Marquess of Douro, his eldest son, has been responsible for running the estate and the shoot. Lord Douro, among his many accomplishments, also chairs the prestigious Purdey Award. About six years ago he reintroduced partridge to the shoot and now a number of partridge days are available both for the family and guests in September and October, switching to mixed days from November onwards. Each year the estate has Mike Swan in from the Game Conservancy Trust (GCT) for a day, half of which is spent on the river and half of which is spent on the shoot. The connection with the GCT is obvious and longstanding as the present Duke was President and Deputy President between 1976 and 1987.

While the keeper is excellent they all find this GCT assistance very helpful. (I recently had Ian McCall up to my new estate, Tressady, in the highlands. Their expertise is vast and worth the money. It is much better to know what will and will not work from an unbiased and knowledgeable viewpoint.)

The Duke is also well known for his strain of athletic and handsome Labradors and he occasionally comes out discreetly picking up a few hundred yards back. A small team of pickers – five or six – are extremely efficient and knowledgeable and most work three to five dogs. The picking team primarily uses Labradors but I also saw some of the best and most enthusiastic golden retrievers running through brush and down drains after runners.

Everything that they do is well thought out and exceptionally generous. They tend to provide more than a brace of bird per gun and all have been beautifully cleaned and packed.

Now here is a remarkable story just to show how uncommercial this shoot is. A team took a day on partridge this past October and had booked a 250-bird day through Drivenshooting. On the day half the Guns were fogged in and could not get down to the shoot. With a team of four guns to deal with, Paul Sedgwick turned to the captain and said, 'We don't believe in counting cartridges here and you probably won't make the bag with just four guns shooting so why don't we just count the birds at the end of the day and I will refund the difference?' Bloody remarkable.

The Team

Headkeeper

Gary Keep joined Stratfield Saye as a trainee keeper in 1988 after studying at Sparsholt College. He worked as an assistant keeper under the tutelage of the late Harry Woodward and then Howard Holloway until taking over as headkeeper in 1996. The underkeeper, John Goodenough, has worked on the estate for two years. He apprenticed at Stowell Park.

Picking Up Team

Bryan Winman has lived on the estate since 1996 and trains the Duke's gun dogs. He is ably assisted by Belinda Routledge, Susette Watts, Tony Sanders and Ray Hardie.

Following publication of my article, I received the following letter from the Duke of Wellington:

Dear Mr Brant,
I enjoyed reading your article about the Stratfield Saye Shoot in the *Shooting Gazette* of May. It occurred to me that you might be interested in why the coverts mentioned in your article acquired their names.

Little Switzerland

Originally the whole of the covert stretched from the main carriage drive and the Wellingtonia Avenue right through to a point in the Park where there is a substantial cottage, which was originally a keeper's. It was a very large piece of woodland, which my Grand-father used to drive with a very large number of beaters. I decided to break it up and make it more manageable for the sort of numbers of beaters we employ these days. The big valley, which runs up through Switzerland, had been cut over during the war and consisted largely of stumps and bracken. I decided to clear this completely and put it down to grass, make a lake from the small stream, which ran down the valley, and rename the woods concerned. Little Switzerland I replanted in a shape more suitable for shooting and we now, as you know, line the Guns up the valley above the lake. I also cut some very big rides in Switzerland itself, which makes it more manageable.

McKenzie's Clump

In about 1900 my Grandfather planted a small clump of Scots Pine in memory of a great army friend of his, Colonel McKenzie, with whom he had served and who had died recently. I therefore planted an extension to the existing covert and since the flushing point was adjacent to McKenzie's Clump I renamed this new bit of woodland McKenzie's.

North End of the Pleasure Grounds speaks for itself and succeeding generations of my family have planted these Pleasure Grounds up with interesting and ornamental trees.

Parkside

This was a small covert, which I planted at the northern end of a very large covert, which we drive into Parkside in order to concentrate the birds and make them fly out over the Park, back to the main covert. As there is a drop in the ground this can produce some good birds.

The stand of poplars shown in the photograph of your article was planted by me for a particular purpose about 40/50 years ago. About 150 yards to the east of these poplars is a covert called Duke's Cedar. This I named after the very large cedar of Lebanon that is at the crossroads adjacent to a flushing point. This was planted by the first Duke on his first visit to the estate in 1816. I planted a covert adjacent to this cedar to take advantage of a slight rise in the ground. The covert is driven towards the river and the poplars were planted on the wet ground near the river in order to make the birds rise before they got to their destination on the west side of the river. It's worked out quite well since the poplars have grown to a good height.

You might also be interested to know that Gary Keep, now the Head Keeper, is descended from a long established local family, one of whom was a bootmaker and claimed to have made the first pair of Wellington boots for the first Duke. I sent Gary, as a boy of 16, to Sparsholt. He then returned to us as a Junior Keeper and now is Head Keeper and relatively young.

I am glad he produced a good day for you.

Ballywalter Park

S ometimes some things are just meant to be.
Lord Dunleath's son contacted me about his family's shoot and its potential
let days last winter. Then his father, Brian Mulholland, Lord Dunleath, took
over correspondence. We struck it off and he invited me to a family and friends'
weekend in late October. Contacting Will Hetherington, who had been here previously, it was agreed that this would make an interesting feature.

The Lord and Lady Dunleath are exceptional people – great hosts, warm and
welcoming – and this was especially important as my wife and I were unknown
to everyone and the other seven Guns, mostly with partners, staying the weekend
were all old friends. This is not to be confused with the type of charming that
normally goes hand in glove with dubious types trying to pick one's pocket, but
rather the innate charm born of breeding. The team and their spouses, in addition
to his Lordship and myself, were in alphabetical order John and Lindy Anderson,
Stephen and Jill Brann, Edward and Blossom Cooper, Ray Entwistle, Capt Noel
Lamb, David and Judy Lindsay, Richard and Rosalind Mulholland, James and
Sorrel Shepherd-Cross.

The first guest that I met was Ray Entwistle. He is an Englishman who has
lived in Edinburgh for many years and former Chairman of the Royal Bank of
Scotland. As I had recently moved to the Highlands, we had much to talk about.
The second couple included a wife who was the step-aunt from a previous
marriage to one of my acquaintances north of Inverness whose family has had
an estate forty minutes' west of our estate for generations.

Lady Dunleath, Vibse to her friends, was a food historian when she and Brian
met six years ago and they have now been married for more than a year.

One of the most unique aspects of the shoot is that the house itself is so
wonderful and shooting guests have the fortunate opportunity of staying here.
The room in which I stayed was vast and very nicely appointed. Paintings and

portraits both large and intimate plus collections from many generations include organs – musical not bodily – taxidermy, antiquarian books and all of those goodies that make a house so special, and it is a special estate that has been the home of Northern Ireland's Game Fair for a number of years. But it is indeed the infectious good humour of the hosts that has turned a great house into a home.

Unlike many great houses it is very much a family home with all that implies. And while it is a home, this magnificently appointed Georgian Italianate palazzo, renovated more than once, with large reception rooms, a great double staircase with a Mander organ on the landing commissioned by the fourth Baron who had an abiding interest in such things, is rather unique. (Except for the cheerfulness of the house, 'The Phantom of the Opera' would have come to mind.) My favourite aspect is the gentlemen's wing with billiard and smoking rooms and conservatory with a glass dome…but enough of the house and history…back to sport!

We had a great feast on the first evening over a dining table a mile long, the meal served by an attentive and efficient staff all trained by Lady Dunleath. Breakfast was typical of a British shoot weekend with relatively little talk, good warming food to sustain us for a day's sport and most gents reading the newspapers provided.

Booting up at the front entrance we walked to the Albany for more java and the drawing of pegs. The Albany was 'originally built as sleeping accommodation for chauffeurs, valets and ladies' maids accompanying visitors staying at the house' as pointed out to me by BD – shades of Gosford Park.

Soon we headed out. The first drive at Kerr's Hill was a combination of pheasant and duck with the duck so tall that none were shot. The pheasant were very good quality but a bit light in numbers due to most of the birds having gone into the next drive at Round Hill.

The second drive produced excellent pheasant out of a very large game crop. The keeper was particularly good and clever: I was to be the gun at the far left of the crescent-shaped line but he realized that the wind was all wrong and had my loader take me around as a back gun. It provided both more shooting and more testing shooting. It is often the case that pegging needs to be changed in this fashion due to wind or other conditions; and I wish I saw more keepers or shoot managers with the conviction to make these last-minute adjustments. Lord Dunleath was also back gunning.

The birds that got past the line in front of me, and they shot very well, provided very good sport – luckily for me there were occasionally too many birds as we were single gunning. I was concentrating well – often an advantage – and had a couple of left and rights in a row and a couple of long crossers as there was no one to my left and no bag constraints. The birds were exceptionally wet and the ground muddy from an inch and a half of rain that fell eighteen hours previously, yet throughout the day we saw very good pheasant.

The third drive again was a combination of pheasant and duck, the duck again being driven and not circling a lake. It provided some very challenging shooting and I shot my longest duck of the year on this drive. A wonderful elevenses was served in front of the manor.

The next drive was primarily duck off a pond in front of the castle with a few pheasant coming out as well. Lunch was back where the pegs were drawn, a buffet of pheasant complemented with excellent wine, fine port and delicious cheese being served.

The fifth and sixth drives near one edge of the estate produced very good pheasant once again, probably the best of the day as it is usually best to end on a high note. The total for the day was 286 pheasant plus seventy-one very good duck. The estate boasts a total of around fourteen drives and can shoot twelve days a season. For those who want two or three days of sport, arrangements can be made to shoot on neighbouring estates or, occasionally, driven snipe at Downpatrick Marshes, which are also in Lord Dunleath's ownership.

Unlike many great houses that welcome shooters merely for lunch this shoot offers the visiting Gun the opportunity to live the Edwardian shoot party life with grace and ease. It does mean a flight to Belfast, which means applying for an additional shotgun permit. Curiously, the Northern Ireland licence is valid for all of Great Britain but a licence from England, Wales or Scotland is not sufficient here. It is a short, easy drive from the airport.

Headkeeper

The keeper, Gordon Wooldridge, originally comes from near Newbury in Berkshire and has been at Ballywalter Park for six seasons. He trained on a number of large estates in both England and Scotland and is excellent. This is not an easy shoot to run in that many of the best drives are near the border of the property, which makes slippage of pheasant quite easy. Instead of using stubble to keep the birds' interest he uses a cattle corn, which he feels keeps their interest longer as they peck at it. He has his own mix of game crop, which he calls the Ballywalter mix, which holds up well. He is helped in his duties by his partner, Debbie, who acts as the underkeeper and who works very hard running around at breakneck speed on her quad bike. Instead of using flagmen exclusively they also have stakes placed between the flushing point and the team of Guns to which she adds some white burlap to flutter in the breeze and help to lift the birds. Beaters generally number around twenty, with a picking team of six to eight.

King Tut's Shoot

For five years, Jim Egan and I shot a few days together each season, mostly in Spain but also a day or two in England and Ireland.

One December he joined me staying at Humewood Castle and shooting at Ivor Fitzpatrick's (Irish) Castle Howard and he reciprocated by inviting me to a day at Highclere Castle. (We are cheesy with Schlösses.) It was a day that appealed for many reasons beyond just the excellent reputation of the shoot. After all, I was a fellow of The Explorers Club by age thirty, the American equivalent of the Royal Geographical Society. While sub-Saharan Africa was my area of interest, the lure of Egyptology always appealed.

The fifth Lord Carnarvon, great-grandfather of the current Lord, funded and was actively involved in the most famous archaeological dig of all time: Howard Carter's discovery of King Tutankhamen's tomb in the Valley Of The Kings. Carnarvon cut a dashing figure as evidenced by a small portrait in the central hall. 'Sort of an Indiana Jones portrait' was how the current and eighth Earl described it; but it displayed, even in that brief glimpse, that he was much more sophisticated and worldly. (Actually it's my understanding that Indiana Jones was inspired by Roy Chapman Andrews, a fellow Fellow of The Explorers Club and a member of Campfire Club. His exploits in Mongolia etc., while on expedition for the Museum of Natural History in New York, from finding the first dinosaur eggs plus fossilized skeletons to being captured by Afghan tribal bandits, are legendary.)

Soon after the Tut discovery, one that appeared both of great importance (correct) and joy (incorrect) for all concerned, the fifth Earl of Carnarvon returned to Cairo. As the story goes he cut himself shaving and nicked a mosquito bite, which rapidly turned septic. (The eighth Earl said 'From all accounts of the man, he probably picked it with a rusty knife,' half chuckling. In either event septicaemia quickly set in and a couple of days later he was telling jokes – one can only presume – with King Tut.)

Death duties and taxes are never pleasant but in lieu of paying them his wife suggested that many important artefacts that were his share should be given to the British Museum. The tax bureaucrats in all their imperious wisdom, aka self-contented stupidity, declined, insisting on filthy lucre solely in terms of coin of the realm. Many of the objects were sold and can now be viewed in New York City at the Metropolitan Museum.

As an anecdotal side note, his son – the sixth Earl – a bit on the superstitious side, kept the pieces that Carter had listed as 'not of great importance' but had them sealed up – entombed as it were – in a hidden room between two others. It was only during renovation sixty-four years later that these items were discovered and they are currently on display downstairs.

Jim Egan had most of his small team of six Guns convene the night before at the Yew Tree Hotel about seven minutes from the shoot. The food was quite good but the bedrooms were bit iffy and very small – sort of like that old joke that one had to step outside to change one's mind. No phone, well-worn towels, plus, indeed, wet towels in the bathroom from the previous occupant and little space to hang one's clothes comprised the digs. Supper, however, was delicious with crusted liver, cold lobster and fish and chips all getting high marks. Breakfast on the other hand could not have been slower arriving, making us twenty minutes late for the shoot. This caused no real problems as we merely skipped coffee before heading out. The price at least was right at about sixty quid including breakfast for two. I guess one does get what one pays for. The best alternative is the Carnarvon Arms, right at the doorstep of the shoot, which was, unfortunately, being renovated.

We were joined by Brian De'ath, Raymond Curtis, David Brittain who owns the Hexton shoot and estate, and Jerry O'Sullivan who had shot with Jim and me at Las Golondrinas. We were merrily greeted by Adrian Wiley who had everything organized to smooth perfection. One never felt pushed, and one never felt about to miss anything either. As we were running late, we chose to skip java and after a quick how-do-you-do to and from Lord and Lady Carnarvon we moved on in a small armada of four-wheel-drives, primarily Range Rovers.

The night before Renata and I ran into an old friend of hers, Anthony Oppenheimer, who shot Highclere the day before and dubbed it outstanding. He shoots enough to know. 'There are four or five other shoots in the locale' he pointed out, in this part of the world, but Highclere, he declared 'the best of all'. He continued, 'The afternoon when the wind picked up, it was even better.' As an historical note of no importance except to myself and friends, Anthony joined us on our first ever day at our pheasant shoot called Shillelagh, where every drive was experimental.

Our morning was hot, humid and still. They were certainly less than perfect conditions, although a few good partridge did come through the first drive, mostly at the lower peg numbers and the ones at the top left (higher numbers) of the drive were most sporty as long crossers well in front. I nearly shot a hen pheasant as I picked up on the movement and was not thinking about the fact that they do put down lots of blue-backs. Fortunately, I pulled off the line just in time. Indeed we saw hundreds if not thousands of pheasants during the day, most of which were already advanced enough to fly well.

'We put down poults very early,' Adrian Wiley had told me previously. Indeed, the Queen takes an October day for partridge and pheasants where she thoroughly enjoys picking up while the male side of the family and guests bang away. This is a very posh shoot as one would expect at the Queen's godson's estate. Indeed, the Duke of Marlborough's sister, Lady Rose, is a regular picker here.

For the record they shoot about twenty-four days per season, generally 300- to 350-bird days, plus two beaters' days where the bags are uncannily big, indeed, formidable. We had four drives before lunch, the last being the best again especially for the low numbers, who had long tall crossers in front of the line. Some excellent shooting prowess was displayed.

Back to Highclere, a building I knew well from the Jeeves and Wooster television episodes featuring Fry and Laurie, where we were joined for drinks and lunch by the Carnarvons. The double library was absolutely amazing; a remarkable room in a remarkable house designed by the same architect who built the Houses of Parliament and it definitely does show. Our bag for the morning was low with only 125 partridge shot by a team who showed exceptional self control as very few mediocre birds had been killed. (As suggested by Sir Joe Nickerson in *A Shooting Man's Creed* – it sometimes makes sense to shoot one's neighbour's bird rather than one's own, if crossers prove more challenging – and we should have cut that deal. After all, forty yards is forty yards.)

A proper staff of butlers, footmen and maids poured Bloody Marys, good fizz, or virtually anything else that guests preferred. The Carnarvons and Adrian Wiley all proved charming and gracious hosts. (They farm roughly 6,000 acres and Lord Carnarvon was very *au fait* with EU directives, subsidies and planning for the farm's future. The Countess of Carnarvon is an excellent designer of women's clothes and is also currently working on a history of the family and the shoot.

The port was too good to pass on, but a small sip sufficed as we had three more big drives ahead. We passed Beacon Hill, the top of which offers views to five counties. On the property are also a couple of lookout posts that were used during World War Two to train bombers to be more accurate. Indeed, there is a field on the estate from which the first de Havilland had its maiden flight.

Also on the way to the first drive we passed Heaven's Gate, the most famous pheasant drive at Highclere, from which all birds shown would have to be cracking – it was just that sort of terrain, which gave no alternative. As we reached the fifth drive of the day the shoot hit its zenith. I, however, needed suntan lotion for my face and insect repellent for my socks but possessed neither. It was bloody hot and still the birds flew fast. As I was at the right end of the line, long crossers to my right escaped without being shot at, protected by a sun that had blinded me in that direction. With clouds and wind it would have been glorious.

The penultimate drive gave us shade from the trees behind and many partridge appeared and while not dramatically high, they were extremely fast; and the low fast bird changing direction can often provide more sport than the slow tall one. It took me this long but I finally started shooting reasonably well, getting in sync with my loader, Les Taylor, who was the loader for the seventh Earl. Along with Wiley, he runs the day, staying in communication with the headkeeper, Eddie Hughes, who has worked on the estate for forty-five years. (This was actually my first day of the season, as my grouse days had been cancelled.) A couple of times I managed three or four birds dead in the air. Bouquets of pheasant appeared and it was a challenge often to pick out the red legs from the blue-backs, which outnumbered them twenty to one during the middle of the drive. Excellent pheasant were shown even though this was only 20 September.

Jim told me of his five great days the previous two seasons, though previously he had only shot in October. Anthony Oppenheimer told me how good his day was on the 19th. Adrian Wiley told me that in all those years only two days had been less than outstanding and this had been one of them. I believe all. We did not beat the birds; the birds had not beaten us. The hot weather and high humidity, on a breathless day, like King Tut, cursed us both.

Total bag for the day was 250 partridge. The shoot is expensive, almost West Country prices, but it is a unique shoot and just a bit over an hour west of London and one is paying for both the convenience and the prestige, and under normal British weather conditions, good sport. Two prices are available; the more expensive by two quid a bird includes lunch in the Royal dining room, the less expensive 'and still jolly nice' as Bertie Wooster would have said, lunch in the Georgian wing.

Cocking

Winston Churchill once wrote that the best passport into society around the world, where one is unknown, is a polo handicap. Today, to be known as being a serious Shot is not far behind.

I had organized a few days of shooting on the Continent for a friend's family shoot a couple of years ago and amongst their friends were the charming, interesting couple Robert and MeiLi Hefner. Urbane, charming and witty, we quickly became quite friendly. While Robert is an experienced and fine shot, he had on order a pair of titanium Fabbris, perhaps the greatest shotguns of all times, MeiLi was relatively new to shooting, so I spent a fair bit of time coaching her. (I must point out that MeiLi has very good shooting instincts. She is an aggressive shot, a distinct advantage, and she is quick and she also takes a hard focus on the target. So I found it quite enjoyable, indeed gratifying, to see her rapid improvement.)

The next year they most kindly invited me for two days of shooting at a shoot that Robert has been taking for the first weekend of November for a number of years called Cocking.

Cocking is in Midhurst in West Sussex. To be honest, it never occurred to me that there could be such a good shoot in the area. While they took two days for shooting and while I was invited for both, I only made the second day, as I was already committed to a team shooting West Molland. On the Friday, Renata and I finished West Molland, skipped lunch and made a mad dash cross-country from Exmoor to the east. We arrived just in time for dinner at the lovely Park House Hotel, which the Hefners took over for the weekend. This is Cowdray country, with its strong links to polo, and while we were not aware of it, strong links to shooting. Renata had rented the Dowager house of Lord Cowdray's when she used to play down here. The Hon. Charles Pearson of that clan owns the shooting, indeed estate, at Cocking and has known Renata for a long time.

To be brutally honest, I thought I was in for a big letdown, heading straight from West Molland Wood, a drive of renown, to Cocking. In fact, the exact opposite was true. West Molland Wood in early November, which shot well, most probably the best of all eight drives shot over the previous two days, was not in fact in the same league as the birds off the fabled Cocking chalk pits. How I could not have been aware of this, I do not know, but my education was both sorely lacking and immediately remedied.

The chalk face, if you have never seen it, is pretty much exactly as one would envisage; it goes up almost vertically, but has three levels on which shooters are placed. Two are on tracks cut into the face and the third, in fact, has double back gunning down below on flat land and Guns placed a bit behind.

The birds coming off the face were stratospheric, providing tall birds even for those guns at the top level. I was on the bottom left peg, very testing sport, which suited me to a T.

The birds that I had on offer were doing many wondrous things and all at altitude. I had birds going from my right to left, *extremely* long crossers, which were dropping and slipping away. I had birds on my right, behaving differently still, and the birds that were straight over head, or close to it, were fifty yards up and motoring. Rarely have I experienced a drive that posed as many different challenges, as many different problems, and as many different sight pictures.

The gamekeeper's son turned to MeiLi and said 'Who's that down in the left-hand corner? He really can shoot,' to which MeiLi responded, that must be Alex. I was in heaven.

Luckily, I had more or less shot every day for the last week and was in top form. Give or take, I was one bird for two cartridges and I was really pleased with myself until I heard that Richard Faulds was on the same peg the year before and reportedly killed forty-eight birds for forty-nine cartridges.

The other three drives we did that day were excellent – certainly the equal of most of the better drives at Chargot or West Molland. I had a great time on all, though on the second drive I was placed as a back Gun behind Robert, who shot so well that I should have taken a nap.

Last year, the Hefners stayed with us at Tressady and shot our first ever day. The sun was against us and the drives did not work as planned. After the shoot they invited me to come down and shoot Cocking again, but unfortunately we had invited our own guests for the following weekend. Renata made me decline – I like being the host but passing up Cocking literally hurt!

Figuratively, I was 'hoisted on my own petard' – for 'petard' translate shoot.

Molland and West Molland

Occasionally a line of Guns unknown to each other comes together in strange and mysterious ways and when it works it is most gratifying. Kirkman Finlay and I had been corresponding for a couple of years since he first contacted me about organizing a shoot for his team to go to Spain. In the end it didn't work out because available dates and his scheduling did not coincide, but being a gentleman of the first order he sent me a box of cigars for the effort and I thought that was a very civilized touch. A friend of mine, FM Claessens, said he would like a couple more days of shooting this season and had a friend to join him for the November days as his guest. Four Guns do not quite make a team unless one is shooting Rothwell. I was a paying Gun as well, the shoot itself had two clients and when Gary Troyer, a doctor from the States, answered a Drivenshooting advertisement in the *Shooting Gazette*, we reached critical mass; Molland and West Molland have a minimum bag of 350 birds per day and that meant fifty birds per man to our team of seven. The two guns who also joined us were Stirling Graham and Adrian Pilcher.

(Note: I am sometimes leery of a review that I write, or that is written indeed by anyone, based on a single day's experience at a shoot. With the exceptions of Drynachan – so disappointing I would not return – plus Chargot and Ballywalter, I have generally had at least three, and more likely ten days' experience, before I consider critiquing a shoot. In statistical nomenclature a single experience is valid, but not necessarily reliable. One really needs to see a shoot over a number of days in a number of weather conditions to get a true feel for its capabilities, strengths and weaknesses. Luckily this report is based on four days at the two shoots on 2 and 3 November and 8 and 9 December. I am very glad that I went back the second time because the differing conditions definitely gave me a much better and more accurate view of the shoot. To make this less confusing for the reader, however, I have written the story as though there were only one team of

Guns while indeed there was a completely different group, with the exception of FM Claessens and Gary Troyer, for the December shoots.)

Both Molland and West Molland shoot four drives a day in normal circumstances. On 2 November, we jumped a bit between the two shoots, although we had lunch at the Lodge associated with Molland on both days. This was done in large part so as to have particularly photogenic drives for 'the snapper', as the editors sometimes refer to them, in this case Jake Eastman. The weather both on this day and the following was not conducive to presenting Molland or West Molland at its best. There was just too much sun and following a frosty start, things warmed up a fair bit. Folly, which is normally quite a good drive, had me at the far right end of the line (number 1) and I had relatively little shooting and at best medium birds. The birds improved to the higher numbers with those at the far end getting some very good shooting. Stacks of birds, mostly partridge, came over the line and to a man everyone showed great restraint, killing only those birds worth shooting. Had they not, a couple of hundred birds could easily have been taken when my guess would have put the number in the cart south of a hundred. The pheasants were much better on this drive than the partridge. The second drive was West Molland Wood, one of the more famous drives in the West Country and deservedly so, the birds were excellent and came at both height and speed. I killed my tallest bird of the day on this drive and must admit I was quite pleased with myself. (It was, unfortunately, fifteen to twenty yards taller than any other bird seen in either of the November days and more what I was expecting as the norm – i.e. big birds.) These were excellent *but not* great pheasant.

My loader for all four days was Phil Llewellyn, who was a most amiable and knowledgeable companion. The 32-gram 6 shot provided by the shoot were not my cup of tea and he organized a good quality 34-gram 5 shot for the next and all subsequent days, which he most kindly had his wife pick up at a shop near their house. As an aside, Phil is shown loading for Mike Barnes on the cover of Mike's book.)

Kerswell, our third drive, was a very pretty setting and perfect for photographing with a lovely stream running behind the line of guns. Some very good birds came out of this drive as well, although it was not on the same level as West Molland Wood. The last drive for the day was Good Heavens and I was at the far left end of the line this time with few birds coming out directly over me. Mostly they were long crossers in front, and those that did present themselves as overhead shots had to run the gauntlet of an exceedingly accomplished team to reach me. While I was a bit out of it, I had four or five truly memorable pheasants killed cleanly at the limit of range to the side – *not in height*, beyond most fellows' view of maximum distance, which made me a very happy man. For the record we shot 206 pheasant and 145 partridge for a total of 351.

On 3 November we shot the four drives known as Trevor's, Pullsworthy, Barn and Pullery. The weather was identical to the first day.

Trevor's showed good birds, but the end Guns, depending on the wind, can be a bit out of it. They double bank this drive and based on the wind, if I were running the shoot, I probably would pull another Gun off the front line based on conditions, especially when teams are small. As we were shooting a team of seven, two or three back Guns could have had terrific sport.

Pullsworthy was another drive that has to be given high marks overall. The third drive of the day, known as the Barn, starts off with a lot of partridge and as it goes on becomes more of a pheasant drive; these were not the tallest birds of the shoot but again conditions might have been against them.

Pullery was nearly a five-star drive with birds coming high and fast and at many different angles. Again starting at one, I wound up on peg seven and had the opportunity to shoot some very, very, very long birds; a brilliant way to finish the day. The bag for the day was 328 pheasants and forty-three partridge for a total of 371.

At Molland on 8 December, Inkwell was an exceptionally good first drive with very sporting birds from one end of the line to the other. At Trevor's I was the left gun at number six (only one gun back gunning), with a strong wind to my right and for the first time in a long time hardly had a single shot; that said the guns on the lower numbers and the back gun had quite good shooting. Badger's Breeze is a drive that they shoot later in the season as they are actually shooting birds pushed from their home woods. Gourt in many ways was the best drive of the day with birds at good height and better speed. The single downside was that it had been shot so often that instead of crossing the line many of the birds were slipping left and right and not going so much over the middle or indeed straight across. Of course, I was in the middle. *C'est la guerre.*

The bag for the day was 277 pheasants and forty-six partridge for a total of 323.

Of all four days 9 December was the best – four and a quarter stars from beginning to end. We started with South Down Wood, which was an absolutely brilliant first drive, indeed, one of the best first pheasant drives I had that year. Fortunately the team was shooting quite well, which made it worthwhile from all perspectives.

Folly had a lot of medium partridge in it but there was an extreme wind and the birds flew like missiles. This was followed by West Molland Wood, which shot better in December than in November. With wind and better conditions (no bright sun), the birds were truly fast and deceptive coming out of the wood. My best bird of the day again was here – five to ten yards higher on average than the November shoot. Again we finished on Pullery, which was a brilliant last drive. FM Claessens shooting on peg seven killed a remarkable number of exceptional birds with his 28-bore London Best choked full in both barrels.

I would have rated the days in November as close to four stars give or take a bit, far better shooting than Chargot but not close to North Molton, Castle Hill or Haddeo. 8 December was very good and had the line men moved a little bit to account for wind etc. on Trevor's – say three back Guns – that day would have been four and a quarter stars too. The following day was four and a quarter stars from start to finish. The bag for the day was 286 pheasants and sixty-one partridge for a total of 347. Still, not quite a top tier shoot.

Molland Estate is owned by Mrs C McLaren-Throckmorton and has been in the family since the 1400s. It is approximately 5,000 acres and contains about thirty drives. They start shooting partridge in September going on to pheasants in mid-October. The best drives include Inkwell, Barn, Curswell, Folly, Trevor's, Dipper, West Molland Wood, Barton, Kingwood, South Down, Pullery, Gourt and Good Heavens. The shoot manager, who is in truth also the headkeeper, is Caleb Sutton who is exceptional at his job and is helped by four beatkeepers – Niel Willison, Robert Luxton, Paul McCarthy and Tomos Bennet – for the shoot. Good elevenses are served, including adequate Spanish champagne/methode, champagnois to be exact. Actually, we had great fizz in November kindly and generously supplied by FM Claessens's guest, Andrew Perryment, whose Range Rover is fitted with the most elegant and well stocked travelling bar I have ever seen. Lunch, however, proved quite disappointing. (Wines were mediocre at best and vegetables quite boring. This could have been remedied with a decent main course, the roasts on prior days were fine, but that was not the case. The lunch on 8 December was, to put it mildly, dreadful. While chicken, pheasant or a roast would have been quite acceptable, they decided to serve lasagne. Now don't get me wrong, I have nothing against lasagne. In fact, a good one can be delicious. Any self-respecting Italian would have committed ritual *seppuku* before serving such a dish. It was mostly pasta, almost no cheese, almost no meat, and zero tomato sauce. I don't know what they could have been thinking. Everyone departed on the 9th before lunch.)

Overall, this was a good experience. The other aspect that they fall down on is that they do not provide shoot transport except for an additional fee the use of four-wheel-drive vehicles. On such a large and successful commercial shoot it would be much more pleasant to have a large shoot bus to take the Guns around so that they could relax instead of having to drive themselves.

Highclere – the team heads out after coffee
and drawing pegs.
(© *Shooting Gazette and Jake Eastham*)

The Duke of Marlborough's sister, Lady Rose,
is a regular picker-up at Highclere.
(© *Shooting Gazette and Jake Eastham*)

Stratfield Saye provided the loader for this Gun who also acted as a shooting coach which is very useful both to Guns who are new to the sport or experienced game shots who are in a bit of a slump.
(© Shooting Gazette and Bob Atkins)

The Guns at Stratfield Saye were served wonderful homemade roebuck sausage with a choice of champagne or King's Ginger and more while they gathered on the terrace. Off to the left the pickers and staff enjoyed their refreshments as well.
(© Shooting Gazette and Bob Atkins)

The author shooting the supremely tall birds of Haddeo – not sure who is more intense, the loader or the author.
(Jake Eastham)

Double gunning is half the fun.
(Jake Eastham)

Without the dedication and enthusiasm of the pickers, the shooting would be much
less fun.
(Jake Eastham)

The dramatic West Country landscape at Haddeo physically forces the birds to the limit of range.
(Jake Eastham)

The odd couple. . .both show great concentration and discipline.
(Jake Eastham)

The downs near Salisbury Plain produce much of the best partridge shooting in the UK and Presscombe is one of the top shoots in the area.
(The Shoot)

Golden retriever in action at Stratfield Saye.
(Bob Atkins)

The Cocking chalk pit provided one of the most exhilarating drives that I ever experienced. Guns are placed on three levels and even for the Guns at the top (shown) they are challenging birds. For those on the bottom level they were simply amazing. *(Renata Coleman)*

Ballywalter in Northern Ireland produces one of the best venues for luxurious accommodation to complement the shoot day. *(Author)*

Our old shoot in the Wicklow mountains at Humewood Castle was known as one of the great duck shoots of the world. The house featured in many movies and on a couple of occasions was the stand-in for Balmoral.

The great shooting house party has survived in a few grand houses even today.
(Top and bottom Renata Coleman)

My loader Phil Llewellyn saved the day at Molland by organizing much better
cartridges than the shoot provided.
(© *Shooting Gazette* and *Jake Eastham*)

Molland: Kirkman Findlay (on right) unbeknownst to me relinquished his gun to the shoot manager. At £40 per bird with VAT, what could he have been thinking?

(© Shooting Gazette and Jake Eastham)

Chargot and one of those magical days of sunshine on virgin white snow.
(© *Shooting Gazette and Renata Coleman*)

Woodcock hold very well for pointing dogs which is the way they are primarily shot at home at Tressady. They also come through the line on driven pheasant and partridge days.
(Nancy Whitehead)

Woodcock are highly prized everywhere and hugely so on the continent with the
French having magazines devoted solely to their shooting.
(Nancy Whitehead)

Guinea fowl basking in the African sun.
(© Gamebirds 2000 world copyrights)

Sand grouse provide brilliant sport especially on evening or morning flights into water.
(© Gamebirds 2000 world copyrights)

Sometimes I think dogs enjoy the shoot day as much as the Shots.
(© Shooting Gazette and Jake Eastham)

Stoke Edith

The drive to Stoke Edith was an adventure in itself. We left our home an hour north of Inverness with the plan of arriving in time for dinner at The Verzon, the hotel booked for the party. After a journey that should have taken us about nine hours, two aspects, neither expected, conspired against us to delay our arrival. The first was the annual sale at the House of Bruar where Renata decided that this was the perfect opportunity for Christmas shopping and the other being horrific traffic jams on the Stirling/Carlisle M80/A80 road due in part to construction.

As the House of Bruar sale was in effect we spent two hours and a bit of money. We did have a light lunch of good soup and acceptable espresso; then we were again, as Renata was driving, airborne. Unfortunately the road across from Glasgow to Carlisle was under construction so we lost another two hours and were quite late in arriving at the Verzon Hotel near Ledbury. We were greeted on our arrival by our most congenial host, Patrick Bookey. Patrick, who is a partner with the St James's Place, had invited us to shoot as his guest at a shoot that I always wanted to try called Stoke Edith. He is a wonderful gentle man, soft spoken and generous to a fault, who not only kindly invited us as his guests but also arranged for a proper coach — Mr Tim Horne — to stuff for and help Renata. Patrick was massively concerned that she enjoyed the day and she did truly love it. The hotel was recently renovated and quite comfortable with absolutely delicious food. While Renata and I arrived a bit late for the proper dinner — we turned up at about 10:30 just as everyone was being served their pudding — they did manage a first-rate, pre-ordered meal for us.

Fortified with an equally good breakfast following a good night's sleep we set off on about a four-minute drive to the Estate. We were greeted by Bob Taylor who acted as host. We had a bit more coffee, seriously more than was necessary, then were given the usual speech on safety followed by the draw of our pegs. Again it was just a short drive to the Quarry where very good birds, especially for an opening drive, were presented. We were all pegged in a long open field with woods in front of us and good birds going over the tops of trees. Renata was a back Gun but with enough birds coming over that back gunning was not second-class sport. She got on well with her coach and shot as well as I have ever seen her shoot on a day of pheasant. It was a drive that everyone enjoyed and the bag on the drive was 106 birds, all pheasant.

The second drive put us on slightly lower ground with a big wood in front and another behind and it was warm enough that the midges were out in serious numbers. I was off to the left of the drive where there were fewer and less testing birds than the right and I believe that this was largely a fact of the lack of wind and the general mildness of the day. I did manage to kill the sole woodcock that I saw on the day and was quite disappointed to see him listed on the shoot card under the rather demeaning moniker of sundries. Eighty-nine pheasant were shot at Dormington.

Bella's Point, the third drive of the day, had a scarcity of birds with a bag of just twenty-six birds but these were some of the fastest and tallest birds of the season. We had a 300-bird day booked and I believe that the drive was chosen because we had nearly 200 going into the drive. I was back gunning and had only a few birds over me but they were screamers and being challenged or beaten actually does amuse me. Like many shoots they save the best drive for last. The Cubwood produced eighty-six exceptional pheasants, all flying high and fast and curling with the wind, which had now picked up to at least a soft breeze. It was actually a long walk down a fairly steep hill to put us towards the bottom of a ravine, the top of which was being driven. (I have also been told that the drive just above this, called Barn Hanger, also produces stunning shooting).

The birds came fast and furious and had they not been quite so challenging, many more than the eighty-six we shot could have been added. The headkeeper is Simon Baker who with keepers Russell Woodward and Lee Alford did an excellent job.

The team itself was quite fun and of diverse background. The gentlemen included a professor of cardiology, a couple of Irishmen (one of whom lives in Yorkshire) and another gentleman who runs both his own shoot and a bird breeding operation. The other Guns included Phillip Stafford, Fintan Cullen, Ivor and Jane Beavis, Mark Brittain, and Prof. Charles McCullum.

Having shot ourselves silly we went back to the shoot lodge for lunch. It was outstanding, the cook Mrs Elizabeth Godsell produced the most delicious roast pork with crackling and first class wines were served to boot. To top it off a '63 Croft came with cheese and while I did pass on the cheese due to high cholesterol, as I was not the designated driver, I certainly did my share of damage on the port. Overall, the experience of the day was exceptional.

Chargot

I was in my New York apartment when I received a phone call from Majid Jafar looking for information on shooting in Ireland. He had read one of my articles and that is how he located me. He was in the States at that time.

A couple of weeks before the shoot in Ireland, Majid joined my team at the king of the Spanish shoots, La Cuesta. The group was small and by the time our three days of shooting was over, we were quite friendly. So it was not too surprising when the following season I found myself shooting with Majid. What was surprising was that it was at Chargot, a shoot that I had never been to. (I had already planned on joining another friend with days at Chargot to review the shoot but among other things, these dates suited better.)

In a funny way, an invite to a famous shoot as yet unseen is like going out on a blind date with someone reported to be beautiful. While she may or may not prove to be so, the image conjured in one's mind's eye and the person in the flesh never quite match.

The drive to Chargot was hairy in the extreme. It was during a so-called blizzard in late November and a delayed ferry crossing to South Wales was followed by a drive over quite icy roads. Arriving four or five hours later than scheduled but still in time for dinner, we found a drawing room full of young adults, most of the Guns about thirty. One or two of the men were a bit older, pushing forty, but at fifty-seven I was definitely feeling the token old guy. This was an international team in the extreme: Alexander Nil known as Tandy from Germany, Carlos Trenor and his wife Natalya from Spain, Joen Bonnier from Finland, Towfik Swaidi, Iain MacPherson, Annabel Nielsen, and the quintessential English gent, Edward Spencer-Churchill.

Had someone been murdered, one would have expected Hercule Poirot to miraculously appear 'just happening to be in the area', to solve the crime. It was a group where everyone was interesting and accomplished. It was just that sort of house party weekend. The first night was casual, the second black tie. Set up in this manner, no one had to make a mad dash from the West Country back to London after shooting on Saturday.

The shoot day was one of these magical days of sunshine on virgin white snow. We all set off to our first drive – Selham.

At Chargot they tend to place rather than peg, which is the better way to do it with an accomplished manager. That said, on the last two drives of the day they had wooden pallets upon which one stood. Chicken wire would have definitely helped to make them less slippery. We were a team of nine and a Spanish-style card was used with various random matrices depending on the team numbers from six to ten. I started on peg seven then went to nine and was second from the end on the third and fourth drives as well. A bit out of it, or rather never really in the thick of it, I still had a good amount of shooting especially during the first two drives.

A game crop up a gently sloping hill put a huge number of birds over the guns on the first drive. Most of the birds over me were in the thirty-plus yard range; and down the line it looked a bit better. A thirty-five-yard bird is a good, challenging target for most guns. I missed the first bird due to bad footwork as it was hard to move one's feet on the slippery *terra infirma* and rainbowed off the line. I killed the next twelve birds quickly and well, each with a single shot, and picked off two pigeons, one of which was my tallest bird of the day. I then got sloppy and shot the next five in the middle rather than in the front. They came down hard but not prettily. I guess I just lost focus. As a Gun said, quoting a shoot manager from North: 'If you kill the head, the arse will die on its own.' Form came and went for the rest of the drive.

The team was shooting extremely well and the Gun on my left, fairly new to shooting though past the novice stage, shot commendably. Intelligently, he hired a coach from West London shooting school to act as his loader.

While I did not time it, the drive must have lasted nearly an hour with good birds and better Guns.

The second drive was similar to the first except birds were not as numerous, though still plentiful. For most of the guns the birds were a bit better as they were pushed over the top of trees between the game crops and the team. These were very good birds indeed, well presented and well shot.

Elevenses were served in the hut, which has a section for the loaders to clean the guns etc. on one side and another for the team of shooters. The two sections are divided by a wall. At the far end of this shooters' domain was a large roaring fire. This is close to the farm building, which is used for lunch; it also makes toilets handy for the distaff half; more shoots need to think of the needs of lady Guns and female companions.

The third drive at my end of the line was marginal and my heart is never in this type of shooting. Indeed, I shot badly. It was after this drive that my neighbouring Gun told me the line about killing the head. Tandy was on the far side and he had what he described as the best birds of the day. From my vantage three of the Guns on my side had middling birds, whilst the rest had really good, challenging sport.

David Powell, obviously being a gent, said that because the team shot so well, the final drive was on him.

The last drive, called *Unbelievable Return*, was not. Light was waning and to be sure good birds were presented but they were not primarily in the forty-plus yard region, which I had expected on a drive with that moniker. I was again perched on a slippery wooden pallet in the middle of a narrow ravine, with moderate trees on either side. It made for a short window, which can be fun, but the slippery pallet encouraged bad footwork on the uncertain perch. That said, I shot reasonably well but it was hard to be quick if a change of body position was necessary for the shot. A fair number of birds stayed with the line of the trees on the far side and while they were quick they were not terribly high, though fairly long. They were dropping and deceptive targets. Those going to the trees behind were much better birds.

The dinner back at the house was excellent and superb wines were served. Chargot is a very well run shoot. To be fair, they did labour under conditions that prevented our reaching some of the drives that they had planned for the day. Indeed, many shoots both on our days and the previous were cancelled because of weather. It is perhaps unfair to give a definitive verdict on a shoot based on one day's sport; nevertheless, it is accurate account for the day. It was, however, a wonderful day, unique in the snow with a super team and all great companions. I had a few tremendous birds over me in the day and I would have placed them at about forty-five yards or a bit more. It was a shame that they were unable to provide their most challenging drives. Had we been able to shoot Melanie's and Spitfire, my view undoubtedly would be altered.

The experience was special for shooting with my host who, with his friends, rates five stars plus.

Chargot – The Facts

The terrain of Chargot, all 4,500 acres of it, was quite as I expected – i.e. typical

West Country topography. (Whereas they shoot over 4,500, I believe they only own 600 or so.) And everywhere were the famous Chargot strips, kale and spring barley, alternating in long rows, typically nine metres wide by the length of the field with three metres open between. Amazingly, they plant roughly 450 acres for use in fifty drives. Four drives per day is the form. There are eighty days per season with expected bags varying from 200–500.

David Powell is the shoot manager and has been for many years. John Marshall, who is a successful businessman, owns the shoot and much of the estate, although he does not own the manor house associated with Chargot. The headkeeper, Nick Boniface, assisted by three beatkeepers (two pheasant, one partridge) and one underkeeper, has been at the shoot for twenty years. The best drives are Spitfire and Melanie's.

Note: Chargot changed hands in spring 2008 but is remaining a strictly commercial venture.

Woodcock at Tressady

No man who has ever carried a gun forgets his first woodcock to the day of his death. You may forget your first salmon or even 'the first kiss at love's beginning', but never your first woodcock: and you may fish, shoot and hunt in any and every land and have the best of sport, but of many days in your sporting diary … the good days with the woodcock will be marked with the whitest pencil and be forever fraught with the pleasantest recollections.

JJ Manley, *Notes on Game Shooting*, 1880. (Personally, I recall the first time I had sex more vividly, but to each his own.)

Wild bird shooting is a sport to be treasured and few wild game birds deserve the respect or show the mystery of a woodcock. While banding studies have given wildlife biologists great insight into migratory patterns of wildfowl, relatively little work has been done on woodcock migration. Compared with a pheasant, who is a short distance sprinter (seven or eight seconds of wing beating and he is spent), woodcock fly across the North Sea from Scandinavia to the British Isles. American woodcock pile up in Cape May, New Jersey, before, when wind conditions are right on a full moon, making the harrowing flight across the Chesapeake Bay.

It is also a bird steeped in literature especially amongst the giants from Russia. Turgenev and Tolstoy both described shooting woodcock in their classic novels.

Shooting woodcock is a truly wild sport for the purist. I always feel a twinge of guilt when I shoot one, and often on driven days, even when it is permitted, will let the cock fly by. Still, whenever one is out on a shoot and beaters yell 'cock', adrenaline flows. In America there are state and federal-imposed limits on migratory birds. In Europe this does not occur and without all the research that needs to be done, one has to use judgement in shooting this small treasure. I do it on our estate by limiting the number of days that we shoot rather than the bag. To my mind a reasonably big bag once a fortnight is probably more fun and of equal damage than shooting the same number of total birds divided over a week or two weeks' time.

I have shot woodcock in Canada, America, Ireland both north and south, England, and in Scotland as far north-west as the Isle of Lewis in the Outer Hebrides. But in my wildest dreams, I never would have imagined that I would wind up owning such a wonderful woodcock shoot as Tressady almost as happenstance.

Serendipity works. When we bought the estate, we were told that it was capable of providing good shooting of perhaps fifteen to twenty-five birds per outing. I must admit that I presumed that number to be high. This year, my first year on the estate with a keeper, we have shot most typically twenty-five woodcock in a day and our best was forty-one over pointers. The number of flushes was great. As I write this, I have just returned from a half-hour outing with my gamekeeper, where *without the benefit of a dog* we flushed thirteen woodcock and four snipe in twenty or thirty minutes. The copse that we hunted was primarily willow spread amongst agricultural land and no doubt the presence of cattle in the fields added much to the invertebrate life that snipe and woodcock favour. This is a satellite wood of perhaps three acres total and half an acre of actual woods that we hunted. We had limited ourselves to this small bit of ground because I had my friends from the roving syndicate from the Brooks's Club up to shoot in a few days and I did not want to disturb the main areas, but rather get a feel for the birds about. Had we a spaniel with us, I would have presumed two or three times as many birds would have been flushed – it was just that casual an outing.

I must admit that the woodcock beat me. I am quite a good shot most days, but being a tall driven bird specialist I am used to moving my feet, planting them and having plenty of time to assess my most difficult target. The woodcock shooting that we experienced was the antithesis of this. It was snap shooting and no warning and coupled with too much choke only a couple of birds came down. We picked them ourselves and unlike pheasant or partridge that I can take or leave as table fare, I am very much looking forward already to that delicious, rich, dark meat that woodcock provide. (I just have to make a mental note to forget that I am eating biologically re-processed worm.)

The quick reflexes necessary for tackling this challenging game bird on uneven ground while off balance need to be honed and practised. I must work on it, or alternatively go out with pointers, which allow one to get set, at least a bit, before the shot. (Woodcock tend to hold quite well for fast-working pointers, which elicit, I presume, predator–prey response.)

The vast majority of the birds that we see in the Highlands are European migrants that have made the exhausting flights from Scandinavia and parts of the ex-Soviet Union. No one knows how many birds winter in Britain each year though I have read that the Game Conservancy is completing a study. Where we live north of Inverness, I do see at least a few woodcock flying across the road on summer evenings, so there must be some breeding going on locally.

That said, and while it is possible for woodcock to come in good numbers in October in some years, it is most typically following the full moon of November that they become abundant in our area. Going out to lamp Charlie in the evenings, I have often seen four or five woodcock in the air simultaneously for their nocturnal movements. (They tend to go from woods to pastures for their night feeds.) Even the great Tolstoy describes evening shooting of woodcock as they travel from their woods to their evening fields. It is exciting shooting as it is difficult to see them and normally one only glimpses them for a moment – a blacker shadow across a dark sky. Fly fishermen who fish after dusk and are aware of bats flying around them will have an advantage in terms of visualizing what this night-time flight is like. Roding is often accomplished down known flight paths, often improved by natural or man-made paths in the woods. Experienced gamekeepers know where to place the Guns for best sport. Anyone who thinks this type of shooting is unsporting or easy has not tried it: try shooting at a shadow some time.

When I first came to Tressady, I tried organizing a couple of days of driven woodcock shooting, but had to relent simply because it was way too dangerous. I have never seen woodcock fly as low coming out of cover. Whether it is because they are recent migrants and tired from their journey across the sea, whether it is the deep bracken that slows them, or whether it is just their nature to fly between waist and shoulder height for a good bit of their travel before rising, I do not know but at Tressady these birds fly so low that only shots behind can be taken and it is nearly impossible shooting.

Having started three driven pheasant shoots from scratch and having reworked a good duck shoot to make it outstanding, it is rather amazing to have a first-class woodcock shoot fall into my lap. It is my plan to do what I can to improve the shooting by strategically planting willows into suitable habitat and shooting areas for woodcock.

Hugh Gladstone, who kept records of such things, noted that a record bag of woodcock shot by one man in one day was 109. Apparently the Gun could have shot more but he ran out of cartridges.

Drynachan – Renata's Birthday Shoot
Highly Overrated – the shoot that is, not the birthday

aving moved to the Highlands exactly a year earlier, September 2006, we thought we would celebrate both that fact and my better half's birthday with a shoot at Tressady.

Tressady had not had a full-time keeper in a number of years and we were not able to find a suitable man until late February so while woodcock, salmon and stalking were all under control, more or less – some pools requiring significant cleaning of detritus to allow us to reach them – his late arrival prevented us from doing enough fox control to take a serious approach to our own driven shoot. We did put a few birds down for experimental days but did not have the confidence to ask our friends to come all the way up from London and its environs solely based on our own shooting.

Renata is one of the sportiest women imaginable: she is one of the few life members of Guards Polo Club where in her heyday she had a two-goal handicap (a big deal for a woman – indeed, for men as well); and for whom, along with Claire Tomlinson and Lavinia Black, the rules were changed to permit women to play High Goal Polo in the UK and Argentina. For a number of years she fox-hunted throughout the British Isles and for six seasons held a Joint Mastership at the Kildares, Ireland's oldest fox hunt. She has recently been invited to be a Joint Master by another Irish Hunt, which I would support if I thought she could afford any more broken bones. Often at our duck days at Humewood Castle and pheasant shoots at Shillelagh, she would run the picking up team while working three of our Labs.

I was indeed right to add a second day as the birds flew in ways we did not predict and did not peg for on our first day at Tressady. Bright sunshine, not a breath of wind and mild weather did not help things at all. While all first days at all shoots are experimental, almost as a tautology, once or twice I have seen everything go to plan on my own shoots on new drives, but most often drives do need tweaking that can only be achieved by trial and error and by understanding the importance of various weather and weather-related factors.

I decided to buy a day at one of the UK's best known partridge shoots just on the other side of Inverness from us called Drynachan. As I have my own booking agency, I approached them early last winter, perhaps even last fall, about sending teams to them for this year. At first they were reluctant, believing that they would fill all their days with repeat business. Come spring I received an email that quite a few days were still available. It was too late to do me any good commercially, since most of my serious teams book for the following year between January and the end of March. While new teams approach me every year, the ones that don't do it early tend to be quite last-minute, those roving or commercial groups suddenly deciding in the fall that they need a day or two more for the current season. I decided that it was too late for me to do anything on a commercial basis with Drynachan, and while their reputation was sterling, I do prefer to see a shoot in operation before I send clients. This enabled me to kill two birds with one stone, as it were.

I had specifically requested in emails for tall challenging birds only. I said I was not terribly concerned about making the bag as long as the birds beat us – i.e. lots of birds at the limit of range. Now I know that a lot of teams claim to be able to shoot high birds, but in the end are clueless. I once had a group from London come to me in Ireland demanding only the toughest drives. If memory serves they had only contracted for about a 250-bird day. I gave them what they asked for and at the end of the day about 210 birds were shot. The team captain asked for a refund at which point I let him know that his team was fifteen cartridges to a bird, which was easy to do with great accuracy as they had bought their cartridges from us. I provided the birds they asked for but I could not kill them for them (actually I could have, but I wasn't shooting).

At the end of the first drive at Drynachan, I spoke to the headkeeper telling him that I was quite disappointed in the quality of birds presented – off a very low, wide tree-covered hillside – as soon as I saw it I had my doubts, which most unfortunately, proved correct. Roddy Forbes, a well known keeper and dog judge, explained that he wanted to see how the team shot. Nothing, unfortunately, is learnt putting birds twenty yards, give or take five, over the line. Personally, I shoot better on forty-yard birds than I do on twenty-five – I rarely raise my gun and if I do so, I do so in a half-hearted manner out of boredom and with a gun that has so much choke that there is no margin of error at that distance. Because

I expected good birds I did not ask the team only to pick the high ones. As everyone was invited, and as no bag limit had been discussed, every marginally acceptable bird was shot at and probably shot. Should a keeper choose this option, it makes much more sense to start guns on birds of roughly thirty to thirty-five yards, and if they can't handle them to go down and if they can to go up.

The second drive was a modest improvement, although for a few of us it was quite a long hike up a steep gorge to mediocre sport. The shooting was more interesting because birds were not in view for very long as they came across the ravine but at least at my peg, and I could only see the peg to my left and right, there were not a great deal of birds and while slightly higher, except for the quickness that was required of the shooter, still not sporting. Casa Sola, an excellent shoot above forty minutes from Madrid near the town of Chinchon, has a drive very similar in physicality where most of the team walks up the side of a ravine. The biggest difference is that at Casa Sola, even months later in March, there are many more birds and at twice to three times the average height. I also find that when mediocre birds are presented or birds in insufficient quantity that many shooters take goofy shots to the side or behind out of range simply to keep themselves amused, which, while it makes the bird cartridge ratio go up, is not a true indicator of the quality of shooting or the Shot.

The next two drives were a great improvement with birds coming off a taller bank. These were the drives with which they should have started. The typical bird was in the thirty to thirty-five yard range, which contrary to most shooters' perception of distance, is a sporting bird for most Guns. A number of birds came off the higher numbers (pegged right to left) with myself at two, which while not providing the best shooting did allow me the pleasure of seeing the entire team in operation. Some excellent shooting was in evidence with most of the best birds over the Guns coming down. The following drive was almost identical. We then had a break for lunch, a picnic really, buffet-style in a fishing bothy on the River Findhorn. It was BYOB (bring your own booze), which at thirty quid a partridge plus VAT was quite niggardly.

The setting for Drynachan is quite spectacular in a typically Scottish sort of way with high cliffs surrounding much of the shooting ground. There is always great joy in a drive with a river as part of the backdrop both from an aesthetic point of view and from the pleasure garnered by watching dogs work in water. (There have been a few drives on a few shoots over the years where the water raged so intensely that the occasional dog was swept away. Just as no bird that flies is worth a man's eye, no bird that flies is worth a dog's drowning.) The Findhorn was low and mild and did not pose any threat.

The final two drives were a huge improvement and quite frankly what I had expected the day to be. Here we were placed in a gully with the red legs stretching the competence of the Guns. While this was late October, and I certainly did not expect the number of birds that one would see in September (my loader telling me that it's not unusual for Guns to shoot 150-plus cartridges on a peg earlier), the birds were still sparse. That said, both the fifth drive and the sixth, which was the return drive, *Cara y Cruz* as they say in Spain, were the highlights of the day.

I had shot with a mixed team that I brought to Spain last year where we were getting absolutely fantastic drive after fantastic drive. Discussing UK partridge, two of the Guns, one a friend who shoots Challacombe quite a bit and another Drynachan, put those two shoots quite high on the list but not up to my Spanish outing. Both are knowledgeable and I believe them both. Is Drynachan capable of producing first-class shooting? Absolutely. Did they on this day? Absolutely not.

Back home at Tressady to shoot the next day, conditions could not have been worse. The keeper, using his limited time, had set the drives all along a long cliff face covered in various levels with bracken, trees, and at the top, heather. In the first drive, even though a sewelling line was employed, many of the birds were below it and took off too low to provide interesting sport. The sun, directly at our back, did not help as well as it will often turn a bird or make them want to duck below. Speaking of ducks, they probably provided the best sport of the day, flying at or above the limit of range to start off the drive, and while only six were killed, they were six exceptional birds. While we had hoped that the partridge would come off the cliff face high, and maintain their height, they flew like traditional partridge, low and hugging the ground with very few as shootable birds – not necessarily because they were unsporting but rather because with a line of beaters on the cliff face above they were unsafe, and happily all of my Guns were both experienced and safe. A few good partridge presented themselves to the last Gun on the left who was able to take them as they turned over his left shoulder as there were no pickers or beaters in the line of fire. Tricky enough shooting – many escaped.

The second drive was at the opposite side of the cliff face and again the birds proved most uncooperative. Instead of crossing the line as we had expected they chose instead to fly parallel with the cliff face, providing good sport on high birds for both end pegs. Strangely, eighty per cent of the birds went over those pegs.

The third drive after elevenses and between the first two had the best show of birds across the line. Woodcock and even the occasional grouse was driven, although none were shot and I don't think any were even shot at. This was followed by a sumptuous lunch and a bit of a rest before the Guns who chose to went out on a successful night flight for wild duck.

The team gathered included Robert and MeiLi Hefner (both shooting), Renata's teenage godson, Adam Coombs, David Nabarro accompanied by his wife Annabelle, Geoffrey Smart accompanied by his wife Margie and his dog Tuffty, Renata and me. The Guns were most kind and generous, expressing their delight in a day that I found most unsettling. Robert Hefner was so kind as to call me to tell me he had never been on a drive like the first where he shot duck, partridge and pheasant all on the same drive. It was different, and it was for me like the Drynachan day, disappointing. But unlike the Drynachan day, as it is my own, non-commercial shoot, it gave me the opportunity to try and rectify some of the problems with my keeper by tweaking the beating, altering flushing points, and changing some of the pegs, as I write this. Tomorrow, I am shooting it again, so the experiment continues.

Happy birthday Renata.

Whitfield

Mike Barnes – (First Published in *Fieldsports*)

We all love to shoot a high bird. To a greater or lesser degree every shoot has them, and estates in Yorkshire, Wales and the West Country, along with one or two other places, have more than most. The great debate is in the equipment used and the ethics of shooting at very long-range pheasants and partridges, but pheasants in particular, which are harder to bring down.

If pheasants cannot be cleanly shot with a modest choked best London gun, then surely there have to be questions raised as to the point of shooting at this kind of bird presentation? And yet we should not forget that Percy Stanbury, whose classical style has been faithfully copied by many of our finest game Shots, used a Webley & Scott live pigeon gun with 30-inch barrels, choked full and full. Therefore if we also enjoy shooting a high bird, then surely we should have the equipment to do so efficiently.

I have kept a pretty open mind on the subject. I have used over-unders exclusively for the last twenty years, purely because they deliver much less recoil (particularly fitted with an Absorball recoil pad) to a dodgy neck. I found that they are also easier to shoot effectively. So that part of the debate is not relevant to me. But is using a 32-inch trap gun with in excess of 40 grams of shot still sporting shooting? On this I have still to be convinced – or at least until now, for I have recently experienced the concept of a day of extreme pheasant shooting.

The destination was Whitfield in Northumberland, a lovely shoot, through the heart of which flows the Allendale river. It was fully resplendent in autumn colour and I was the guest of Dave Carrie, from North Yorkshire, who in light of the current debate, had invited me to see a full day of seriously high pheasants. His Magnificent Seven team were equipped for the occasion with 32-inch guns and loads ranging from 34 grams (in a 20-bore) to 50 grams (in a 12).

Unfortunately, due to a late cancellation, there were only six Guns (another member had to leave at lunch, leaving only five), but for the purposes of the day it mattered little – they got more shooting and I got my story.

Dave, fifty, who runs a successful waste business near Leeds, explained that he didn't discover shooting until he was thirty-seven. But he has since made up for lost time. He is an outstanding shot and is the current GB FITASC Grand Prix champion. His passion in all forms of shooting is 'long birds'. So much so that he shoots exclusively on high bird shoots in Yorkshire, Northumberland and Wales. Whitfield is a particular favourite as they offer a day of Extreme Pheasants, during which all birds will be at forty to seventy-five yards, with many more distant still.

We met the night before at the incredibly accommodating Centre of Britain Hotel in Haltwhistle, where Dave explained:

> People don't think it is possible to shoot birds at seventy to eighty yards, but tomorrow with the right equipment I think you'll see that this isn't the case. And as for wounding or damaging birds, you will see less of that than on many normal shoots. I will be using 50-gram loads of 3 shot. They carry 210 pellets and with full choke there will be enough in a group of sufficient impact (due to the size of the shot) to be effective and kill the birds cleanly without damaging them.

He added that he normally used 42 grams of 4 shot (both by Express), but for the purpose of these words chose 50 grams to show what was possible. He quite fairly made the point that this was no different to using a 6 shot pellet for half the range. 'We are using loads that are considered normal for wildfowling, but as we are shooting pheasants at ranges typical for wild duck, then there is no difference.' It's a fair argument, and one that makes more sense as the day unfolds. As it transpires he is one of three British champion clay Shots in the line who regularly shoot with him at Whitfield – John Hargrave from Spalding, Lincs, uses a Kemen 32-inch choked full and super full, with the same Express Max Game 50-gram loads, while former British Open champion Tony Booth, from South Yorkshire, like Dave, shoots a Miroku 32-inch but with Saga 44 grams of 4 shot. The other regular member of the team is Tom Bailey of South Lincs (a former county champion) who uses a Browning 20-bore with FOB 34 grams of 4 shot. Joining them was retired Lichfield lawyer Graham Moore, who shoots a Fabarm 30-inch over-under choked full and three quarters. He shot some home loads, 42 grams of 3 shot provided by David Whyte (loading for Tom), and then Express 32-gram 4 shot and 36-gram 5 shot.

Just two drives occupied the morning. I stood behind Dave on peg one of Craghead. He was accompanied, as usual, by Desmond Mills, a retired ex-Purdey gunsmith who lives near Harrogate. 'Des is a very good loader and we work really well together. I have no sight in my left eye, so he watches to my left, which leaves me free to concentrate out front and right.' The pegs are among rocks at the water's edge, the birds being driven over the tall trees that cover the sharply rising cliff face of a bank opposite. Their tops are eighty yards distant. Odd birds appeared down the line and eventually in front of David, but as is often the case on an end peg they were veering off to the right, making for very difficult shots. High, crossing, curling, gliding, dropping – and a long way away. His first four or five shots brought no result, none too surprisingly. But there was no panic, the motion was smooth, no snatching, no quick shooting, just sure and deliberate. Then he found them. It was quite incredible – he was pulling off some amazing shots, birds that us lesser mortals would not even consider as 'in range'. Yet he clearly knew he had the capability – and like anyone in sport who is good at what they do, he seemed to have lots of time.

Next peg down, John Hargrave was similarly plucking some spectacular cocks out of the heavens. The birds were more directly overhead for him. In fact, looking down the river it was possible to see all enjoy some fantastic shots, Tony Booth accounting for a hen with ice on its back.

The drive was meticulously run, with pheasants dribbling out over all of the Guns, then there were pauses, a few more, then a small flush. 'The hardest part is looking up,' Dave turned and smiled. I too was craning to stare at the tree tops. Then a cock soared high overhead. He killed it beautifully, before he swung onto an enormously long hen making its escape along the tops, left to right, which he shot as clean as a whistle. It must have been close on ninety yards. Amazing. A fantasy right and left.

But he hadn't hurried, he had chosen his bird, as Stuart Maughan says:

The secret is in studying the bird. People can come here and easily get disheartened. Very often they miss a bird and then start giving ridiculous amounts of lead – but as in all game shooting no two birds are alike, just as no two days are alike. What you have to do is study the bird and think about it – what is it doing? Look for the line. You know you have the equipment – you just need to put it in the right place.

While very, very few shoot consistently here, this team clearly get it right more than most. The second drive was King's Wood Rock, a jewel in the Whitfield crown. Guns were this time stood with their backs to the river, the sharp tree-covered escarpment running up in front of them.

I stood with Graham Moore, who was back Gun and shoots with the team from time to time. He is also a regular at Brigands in Wales. 'I am not in the same league as these boys, but I enjoy shooting with them here. They are very, very good. The whole day is quite demanding, but I love a challenge and my view is that you only get better through experience.' With that, he shot a high cock to his right, a lovely bird and a great way to start a drive. 'The only drawback to these kinds of days is, camaraderie apart, they make some other shooting seem a bit mundane!'

I could see the others pulling down some fantastic pheasants, and a number out front too. Dave later explained: 'You don't want to rush your shot, but if they are coming directly overhead, I tend to think in terms of my shot charge meeting the bird head on – it has to make for an effective shot, and a greater chance of a clean kill.' He gave the broadest of smiles, which was, in fact, the most regular occurrence of the day all along the line. 'Well, what do you think – is it what you imagined?'

He knew the answer to the question. Likeable, enthusiastic, and an incredibly good shot, here was a man in his element. I had seen what the helpers on the shoot had seen – a team who could handle themselves. They were clearly very good and very experienced. They knew what to shoot, and what not to shoot. In other words – sporting. And me? I'm not sure I could handle this equipment, but if my neck would permit it then I wouldn't now have a great deal of hesitation. An old Guinness catchphrase came to mind. It ran along the lines of 'I don't like Guinness because I have never tried it.'

There has always been shooting at Whitfield but it was not until 1989 that the transformation started. Headkeeper Stuart Maughan has been instrumental in establishing it as a premier league shoot.

'I joined as an underkeeper in 1976,' Maughan told me, 'straight from a year studying gamekeeping/fishery management at Sparsholt. Born in Carlisle, I had always loved the grouse moors, but after leaving school qualified as a teacher and taught history and PE at Ashington, from where I now get all my beaters.' The call of the wild was irresistible and he gave up teaching to go to Sparsholt College in Hampshire. 'It was excellent and I learned a lot – I also got to meet the legendary Harry Grass, the Broadlands headkeeper, who was very good to us.'

Having joined Whitfield, Maughan found it practically going backwards – there were only two keepers on 16,500 acres, including a 6,500-acre grouse moor.

I very nearly went back to teaching. But when John Blackett-Ord took over in 1989 we had a good chat. I felt that we had a beautiful estate, which we were not utilizing. Thankfully he was as keen as I to create something special. He agreed and to his credit made a big investment and we have never looked back.

They have certainly fulfilled their ambition. There are now eight keepers, two of which are full-time on the moor, which has this year delivered 2,100 brace, while the partridge shooting off cover strips and moorland edges has gone extremely well, and now they are all but fully booked for their magnificent pheasant shooting by the Allendale river.

None of the river drives that have become such hallmark of Whitfield existed prior to his time. There are now twelve high drives, the most famous being King's Wood, Craghead and ERII. 'We only do ERII a few times a season – in this way we keep it special.' The birds are in the woods, where they are hopper fed. 'There's no hand feeding – the hoppers keep them wild. The only problem is that you never quite know what number of birds we will find in a wood on shoot day.' That is why he doesn't peg out, but positions Guns according to how the birds are flying. The pheasants are released as poults, so that the keepers are free in spring and early summer for vermin control.

They offer three types of day – Extreme, Intermediate and High. Charges are based on shots to kill ratios.

For an Extreme bag of 225 we give 7:1, but usually ask for eight double Guns. Realistically, it works out 10+:1. On this particular day it was 1,930 shots for 203, though David, John and Tony would have been well below that figure.

On Intermediate and Valley Partridge 4:1 (more often 5 or 6:1) and High (which is a mix) 5:1, normally 7:1. The purpose of us giving cartridge rates is to cover ourselves for selective Guns who shoot at the best and miss but do not take on more reasonable birds. Prices per bird reflect the bag size and amount of shooting.

I like all Guns on all days to fire a minimum of 100 shots per day but an eight-Gun 250-bird day on Intermediate would work out at 150+ on average. On Dave's day it would have been nearer 300+ as we were only six Guns, dropping to five. On Extreme it would normally be 200+ each per day.

Loads vary, but this team were using 42-gram to 50-gram loads from 32 inch barrels with 3–5 shot and full choke and are good shots, if not some of the very best. Not many can stand this level of firepower. On average 32-gram to 40-gram is the norm with 4–6 shot, but everyone has their own choice of load.

We put the birds over in and out of range and let the Gun choose what he shoots at. If he thinks it is too high he can leave it for a lower one, which is a choice many shoots are unable to offer. I struggle with high bird critics who I presume require little challenge, often no better than 2:1 and like large bags of birds at twenty metres or less. I see most birds wounded at the closer ranges when the Gun is perhaps just not fully on them.

High bird shooting is not for everyone and some get very frustrated at missing, but most sportsmen thrive on the challenge. It takes time to reach this level of skill and the right equipment helps, however one of the best birds I ever saw shot was with a 24-gram 20-bore. I have seen some immense birds shot by experienced Guns over the years with a variety of gun calibres, chokes and cartridges.

They run a strong team of pickers-up to monitor wounded birds and sweep the area well afterwards. 'We try to run eight or more pickers-up who know the ground. We sweep the ground and use radios to pinpoint a picker-up onto a bird he may not have seen.'

Their returns confirm their shoot efficiency – forty-five per cent on pheasants and sixty-plus per cent partridges. No doubt their topography also helps, in as much as over rolling hills birds glide into the distance, whilst here over these steep valleys they either land after clearing the tree tops or pitch into the wood. They don't shoot big bags but Stuart has no objection to them: 'I am against the large-scale shooting of poor quality, but bigger bags are fine if they are good sporting birds.'

Holkham Hall
John McCloy II

When one conjures up visions of England during the heyday of the blood, there are a number of images that immediately leap to mind. Aside from the most well known and frequented tourist attractions, some of the most mind-bending sights imaginable are the great country houses that populate the British countryside. Sandringham, Blenheim, Hever, etc. are homes that can only find comparison in the United States in some of the 'summer cottages' of Newport and even then the disparities are as wide as the Grand Canyon.

One of the greatest of these English estates is Holkham and its magnificent Hall, long the home of the Earls of Leicester. Seated in the middle of a seriously substantial estate, the Hall is both overwhelming in its sheer size and in its grandeur. This 25,000-acre estate has been home to the Leicesters since the middle of the eighteenth century and is dominated by an amazing Palladian mansion, undoubtedly one of the greatest of the great homes of England.

On approaching the Hall the dilemma is discovering the entrance to the extraordinary edifice. On either side of the building are facades that are intimidating while the entrances themselves are surprisingly modest. One can imagine the architect purposely designed it this way as, once through the door, the visitor can only gasp in awe. The main staircase is beyond description as it soars in splendour above the onlooker. It is large enough for the Earl of Leicester to hold concerts of considerable size.

Needless to say, the main rooms and hallways rival the entrance hall and if one can recover from the stunning overall experience, the art that populates the walls and niches is in every instance of museum quality. Rubens, Titian, van Dyck, Poussin, Audubon (a full portfolio), Lorrain, Gainsborough and Canaletto are but a few of the artists whose works adorn the Hall. Were that not enough,

Roman and Greek statuary, mosaics from Hadrian's villa, books and hand-illustrated manuscripts, silver of unimaginable beauty and volume, tapestries, etc. proliferate every conceivable space.

The central reception rooms are surrounded by four wings. One houses the chapel, another the rooms where the Head of State would reside were he or she to visit, the Stranger's Wing where people as fortunate as we have laid our heads to rest and finally the Family Wing, which is occupied by the Earl and Countess of Leicester. This wing contains the owner's bedroom, an intimate dining room for smaller groups and one of the most beautiful libraries I have ever had the fortune to enter. Once upon a time, not long ago, it housed the Leicester da Vinci Codex, which, after passing through Armand Hammer's ownership, is now in the William Gates collection, who upon gaining possession reverted its name to the name it had long held, The Codex Leicester.

Enough description of the Hall as anyone wishing more can find volumes of information virtually anywhere as this is considered one the truly great homes in England. Any description of the Hall, however, would be sorely remiss without a word or two about the Earl and Countess of Leicester. Two lovelier people do not exist. Not only is everyone accepted and treated as a close friend but every need or wish is attended to by Lady Leicester and her staff. She has worked long and hard to renovate and functionally modernize what was always a magnificent edifice into a warm and loving home. Lord Leicester is not only the consummate host but, since he inherited the estate, he has transformed it into a highly successful agricultural enterprise. A daunting adventure considering the state and size of the estate he inherited.

While truly great and important houses are rare in and of themselves, great, entirely wild bird shoots are even more so. When both are offered in tandem, one has the makings of not only uniquely special sport but an overall experience for which this Gun can find no comparison.

Now to the shooting. If one is lucky enough to be invited to live in the Hall itself, breakfast before the shoot is buffet-style with no want for anything that one's heart might desire. It is generally in a ground floor room accessed via a labyrinth of hallways and stairs. To the initiate finding one's way from the Stranger's Wing is a daunting undertaking. After having had the pleasure of shooting here and staying in the Hall over a great many years, my wife still finds it remarkably easy to become lost. Following breakfast is the usual scramble to get equipment together, haul on boots and rush to the courtyard to draw for pegs. Once accomplished, the Guns pile into an elongated jeep-type vehicle, chauffeured by His Lordship, and it is off to the first of the many beats.

While driven shooting undoubtedly began on the continent of Europe, the battue as it was called in France, it was in England that the sport was brought to its pinnacle. Holkham was critical in establishing this paradigm….

Holkham, (is) the great estate on which many subsequent shoots were modelled. There, in the probable birthplace of (English) driven pheasant shooting lives the family whose passion for sport has frequently been stronger than the attraction of fashionable society. True, there have been many famous visitors to Holkham; but the owners, the Cokes, Earls of Leicester … have been able to concentrate on innovation in both sport and agriculture.

(The above is from the first edition of *The Great Shoots* by Brian P Martin, a book which the author heartily recommends.) The independent spirit of the Cokes of Norfolk is exemplified when, during the American Revolution, the resident Earl was known to toast George Washington rather than his King.

One must remember that all the birds, pheasants, ducks, partridge and, of course, woodcock are entirely wild. A few reared birds are released in the Park each year to ensure that the wild birds do not wander off. While the wall surrounding the Park is 9.5 miles long, the Park constitutes only a minor part of the estate. Outside the Park every bird is wild and since the entire estate comprises 27,000 acres there is plenty of room for wild birds. One cannot expect a 'high' volume day but in almost every beat the birds are challenging and in enough volume to make any reasonable Gun happy. Double gunning is not usually permitted by the Earl. As a result one has birds constantly in the air and enough escape even the best of shots to ensure more days of great shooting. On 'cocks only' days, His Lordship does invite his guests to take a crack at the occasional hen 'should she particularly please you'.

Much of the land owned by Holkham is outside the Park and is less heavily wooded than the acreage within the vast wall that surrounds the home farm beats. Both offer excellent shooting though the woodcock tend to seek the cover provided by the forest that is more prevalent within the wall. During the year the Earl has a very few days of partridge shooting and is it is offered only when there are plenty of them about. Again this is to preserve the wild stock.

The first Lord Leicester was the son of the great Coke of Norfolk (pronounced 'Cook') who was granted his Earldom by Queen Victoria. Lord Leicester was a country gentleman and is credited with understanding driven birds better than almost anyone of his era. Someone said of him, 'no one knows better than Lord Leicester how to make pheasants do what he wants them to. His knowledge of the birds and how to persuade them is so great that it is quite possible that he might be able to achieve what has always been credited to his powers – drive them into his billiard room.' When the third Earl's wife died in 1931 she was to be laid to rest in the family cemetery. It was discovered that two pairs of partridge were sitting on nests on or close to her gravesite. Therefore, Lady Leicester was literally put on ice until the chicks had hatched and had left the cemetery. Holkham had coverts planted in the early 1800s, which were designed for sporting purposes. Thus as driven shooting was getting into its heyday in the Edwardian era Holkham was in a grand position to provide brilliant sport. It and Elveden were two of the most important shoots during the heyday of the Edwardian house party and remain so today.

In many articles there are detailed descriptions of each individual beat or drive including comment on whether one drive is better than another. Having shot at Holkham for over twenty years, I can safely say that from year to year the quality of the birds in one drive or the other depends on the wind, the weather in general and where these wild birds might decide to gather on any particular day and I will not bore the reader with such recitation. Far more important is the company one keeps on these memorable days. Without exception the guns and their companions who are invited to attend are peerless. They are invariably fun, interesting, attractive and warm – a great tribute to our hosts.

Nevertheless, that having been said one cannot write any comment about shooting at Holkham without mentioning two beats in particular amongst a host of great drives. Joe's Stop, an isolated clump of trees, is the first. Here the birds are pushed into a stand of trees in the middle of vast open fields that are alternately planted with sugar beets or other crops, all of which are not only designed to provide revenue for the estate but also to hold birds. Once gathered in the Stop, the birds are driven to the Guns, who are lined up along a front of trees at a considerable distance from Joe's Stop itself. By the time the birds reach the Guns they are flying at serious height and even more speed. The trees behind the Guns force the birds to find elevation and the terrain gives every Gun very good sport – that is if you manage to hit what is presented.

The other drive I would like to mention is Scarborough Clump, which is reputedly the place that the first pheasant was ever driven in England. This again is much like Joe's Stop but the mere fact that one is standing where history, from a shooting perspective, was made adds an aura to the moment that this Gun for one never fails to recognize. I always offer a prayer of thanks for the privilege I allowed to savour. The birds are high, fast and well spread.

Finally one needs to mention that during the latter part of the season, the woodcock arrive in droves from Scandinavia and no drive passes without at least one woodcock bursting from the dense underbrush and weaving its way past the Guns. As the woodcock are migratory and since weather conditions dictate their arrival at Holkham, the eastern most point of land in the United Kingdom, there will be times when they are relatively scarce while at other times they are so plentiful as to practically rival the cocks in numbers. I can recall one drive a few years ago when in one drive I was able to bring down eleven woodcock as well as a few very good cock pheasants. Clearly it was one of the more memorable moments in my shooting career. (By the way, Holkham now also offers pure woodcock days.)

Elevenses do not exist at Holkham unless the sleet and snow are horizontal and the temperature is freezing. The Countess then takes pity on the Guns and provides soup and sausage rolls, much to the Earl's fury. He advises the Guns that they are 'here to shoot' and not to take coffee breaks. Lunch is served in several venues. One is in a folly built on the lines of a very lovely Grecian temple. Another is in one of the gatekeeper's houses, which the Earl of Leicester converted to a cosy, comfortable retreat when he and Lady Leicester occasionally needed to escape for a day or two from the immensity of the Hall. Tradition has it that at the end of lunch, the shooting party is offered a raw onion in a box that has been passed down for generations. While some politely decline the host remembers those brave souls who partake.

Returning to the Hall after the shoot, all the Guns repair to a ground level room replete with a great fire, newspapers and a sumptuous tea loaded with all the goodies that none of us have any right to eat and enjoy according to any doctor one might wish to consult. It is a relaxing down time and allows a few tall tales to be broached and boasted about.

Dinners are always black tie with the ladies dressed in their finery. Cocktails are in the library and are relatively short in duration as the excellent wines invariably served at dinner, should not be tainted by too much whiskey before-hand. The library itself was once described by Nigel Nicholson as 'the most beautiful room in England'. Many is the time when dinner is presented in the main reception room with an impossibly long table adorned with hundreds of candles reflecting off more glorious silver than one can grasp. The food is always outstanding and far too much wine is consumed. At the end of dinner the ladies repair to another room while the gentlemen settle into a good cigar and excellent port, always ensuring that it moves properly to the left. Once rejoining the ladies there might be a brandy or some similar beverage for the heartier souls and then it is off to the Stranger's Wing to sleep the night away in impossibly comfortable surroundings.

Should one not be fortunate enough to live in the Hall, very near the main entrance is a very attractive inn called The Victoria, which Lord Leicester's son, the Viscount Coke, renovated just a few years ago. The Viscount now manages the estate and lives in the Hall while Lord and Lady Leicester have remodelled and live at Model Farm, a lovely house on the estate from which they can still lend their advice and help to ensure that the business and sport that distances Holkham from most of the rest continues to flourish.

Headkeeper

The headkeeper is named Lester (different spelling to be sure) and has a large team of underkeepers. All wear bowler hats which form a shield that they can lower when having to plough through dense thickets. In fact the bowler hat was invented by the Holkham keepers many a year ago. The hats were discovered by the guests that came to stay and, impressed by their usefulness and looks, they transported them back to London. Beaters are plentiful as well as an impressive number of pickers all equipped with well trained dogs. A serious effort is made after each beat to ensure that every bird downed is picked. A tour through the Hall and the Museum is worth every minute.

Stanage
Clinton Smullyan

All good shots are pleased when they are shooting well and the birds at which they are shooting survive unscathed. The high, fast, windblown pheasant at The Stanage Estate offer the opportunity to miss well on numerous occasions in dramatic settings. But that comes later.

For seven years, we have arrived at the gates of Stanage Castle on a Thursday afternoon in November in a variety of transport. One of our syndicate consistently arrives in a vintage Rolls or Jaguar or a rather Bondish Aston Martin DB5A. Others in Land Rovers, and others, your author included, arrive collectively in a modest hired coach from Craven Arms, a nearby village. However transported, arrival at Stanage is transporting.

Through the gates, away from anything resembling the twenty-first century from which we have travelled (cherished friends, long time shooting companions, have come from London, Paris, New York) we stand on the gravel of Stanage Castle's courtyard looking over woods and vast fields littered with lowing sheep (more on them later) and wandering pheasant, with nothing else but wooded hills and sky in view. This is, I am told, the least developed area of England, near Knighton, with the Stanage Estate running along both sides of the border of Shropshire and Wales. On many drives, a bird shot in Wales lands in England, and vice versa. Pheasant are no respecters of political boundaries.

To greet us are the owners of Stanage, Sophie Coltman-Rogers (lovely, warm, diffident, with layers of charm, grace and personal delights to be discovered, year by year) and Jonathan Coltman-Rogers. Jonathan is ranked as one of the finest shots in England, and, although *The Field* has not yet published a list for this characteristic, he would certainly rank as one of the most amusing. Together they not only look the part as if sent from central casting, but are genuinely the perfect host and hostess for an Edwardian country weekend. Although these are let days, we have come to feel as if we are welcome guests, indeed, as a romantic notion, we are Edwardian guests, but with better plumbing and heating. Perhaps in the second edition of this work the publisher will allow the Coltman-Rogers to express their own opinion of our guesthood, but for all these years, the willing suspension of disbelief has served us admirably.

To understand Stanage, one needs to know of its 'modern' history, which is to say, since 1800. Jonathan's family has owned the property since dinosaurs roamed Shropshire, or, at least, since before this castle was completed in 1809. It is perfectly natural to wonder why a Regency house would be called 'Stanage Castle'. The crenellated days of needing merlons and embrasures for the bowmen and sally ports for the knights in armour were long gone by 1809 in England.

But, the early nineteenth century was a time of fierce battle between the age of reason and the age of romance. Although written a little later, think of *Wuthering Heights* – Catherine's romantic love of Heathcliff, the brooding, handsome windblown fellow, as against her marriage to Edgar, the stable, conventional orderly man. Ordered gardens and ordered lives were battling for ascendancy with romantic naturalism and true love – in art, literature, architecture and quotidian life.

Jonathan's ancestors hired the very prominent Humphrey Repton to improve the Stanage property. Repton was a follower of Capability Brown in landscape design and believed in the interpretation of nature that included ruthlessly imposing the romance of the 'natural' on landscapes that were insufficiently so (imagine ripping out a mature pine tree at the edge of a pond to install a mature weeping willow – far more visually romantic, as nature 'should' be). Eventually, Repton began to design the houses that were placed in his landscapes as well. In many of his efforts he first created what we would think of today as a marketing brochure to convince the owner that the work was necessary and would result in greater beauty. These 'red-books' (for the colour of the binding) were constructed of drawings with tissue overlays to display the before and after visions of the landscapes. Most red-books are lost, or in museums or private collections. A very few, like Stanage Castle's, are still wonderfully ensconced in the houses for which they were drawn. And that is why Stanage is a Castle, because Repton used the architectural vocabulary of the Ancient Castle as a romantic folly to wrap the gracious proportions of its Regency rooms.

Some years ago *The Field* named the ten greatest shoots in England. For nine of them the text extolled the land, the birds, the keepering and the shooting. For Stanage, the text mostly described the wonderful comestibles. One eats very well indeed at Stanage, in a beautiful dining room, which, seating our sixteen plus the Coltman-Rogers, remains quite spacious with room for more. Furniture, pictures, china and table settings are all traditional and of high quality. Wines are French, generally claret, well chosen and very good quality indeed. Every bit of food, from *hors d'oeuvres* to *chef d'oeuvres* of the various courses, is splendid. Enduring group favourites tend to be at lunch in an ancient schoolhouse: the perfect British preparations of sticky toffee pudding and game pie. Breakfasts are British traditional – one can feel oleaginous delights moving viscously through the arteries towards the heart – and dinners are sophisticated, complex, scrumptious and artistically presented – often an eye-popping exhibition of palette and palate.

So that's the setting. At 9:15 Friday morning we are out front choosing pegs for the first drive. I send a short prayer skyward to draw a peg that is not between the two superb shots who believe birds in front of me are of the greatest possible interest; one of these men I have been shooting with for over thirty years, and I pay for it whenever he is alongside. To his benefit, he shoots at his skilful best when taking my birds and it can be a pleasure to watch (and to enjoy the opportunity he thus presents me for birds in front of him). The draw, and, Success! I will be surrounded by gentility and well positioned for any of the twenty-five or so drives at Stanage.

The first drive of the day, Riverbank, is the opportunity to get one's eye in, between a railroad line and a stream on the Shropshire-Wales border; hastening, we must cross the train tracks towards the stream bank where we line out and wait until the day's only scheduled train, one small rattletrap carriage, has passed. Somehow that toy-like display of railroading is the most convincing aspect of the rurality of our location.

This drive behaves differently each year – last year the first third of the drive was partridges flaring out of the wood atop the high bank in front of us, grabbing the crossing wind and whipping downstream over the lower pegs. This year it is bouquets of pheasant presented over the middle of the line. And then, partridge and pheasant over the whole line. These are the most approachable birds on the shoot, twenty to twenty-five yards up, building our egos and our confidence for the next drive. As with many drives at Stanage, Guns at one end of the line or the other are moved as the drive matures, making it harder for the wiliest birds to evade the line.

A wonderful drive follows at Lurkenhope (where did they get that name?), definitively testing high birds at one of the glorious view corridors that makes up Stanage, but the line is up to it, shooting is good. Then, of course, elevenses, since

Stanage never lets a full two hours pass without our consuming something reasonably unhealthy and invariably delicious. Traditional bacon butties, sausage rolls and other artery cloggers are served with broth, sherry and a bitter liqueur made from one of the local berries. I note that no one who actually lives in the area will drink this concoction, so I abstain, mostly, as others pretend to be intrigued by the corrosive distillation tasting distinctly of cough syrup and battery acid.

Then we are at Guys, where the beaters bring in a vast acreage over the top of a cliff-like structure facing the Guns, its upper slope carpeted with scrub and heather, and, behind the line, a steep, wooded drop-off to the valley. These birds are high and fast and often untouched by the lead cast about them. Pickers-up are placed well behind the line, some several hundred yards, to retrieve birds shot overhead. Even birds killed well in front are often picked up well behind as wind and height and set wings carry them down slope. There are several drives on this side of the property and all share the characteristics of gorgeous scenery, tricky wind, imposing escarpments from which the birds are driven, and birds that are at the very edge of range. Some are beyond range, of course, but the brilliant keeper, Rob, seems to be able to keep the birds at a height where we do not have to select the truly challenging ones, because there are no others. In this line, gentlemen and ladies all, we are delighting in the birds that get away. Remarkably, we hardly ever see a low bird on most drives and when the occasional one is shot, it invites impolite expressions of disdain from the line.

This year we have three ladies shooting. We do not expose them to those among the loaders who can recount for hours without repetition the variegated local jokes that are populated with sheep and Welshmen; it is, of course, the Welsh loaders who are the best at this infinitely contorted, inventively unlikely biological humour (ask for Phil). All the men learn to say, in case of being found out, 'No, Darling, I thought that was very tasteless and not funny at all. I was guffawing to be polite.' We are careful in our further dissemination of sheep-based humour, not least because the ladies shoot damn well and each corresponding spouse can easily imagine himself a target.

Then to the schoolhouse, old, wood-beamy, redolent of smoke and spices, for luncheon, a model of disingenuous restraint with a powerful undercurrent of both gourmet and gourmand – game pie, sticky toffee pudding, gorgeous Shropshire blue and Stilton cheeses. Laughter and compliments for particularly notable shots. Properly insincere humility. And, of course, access to the loo, the primary mandate driving the choice of a break for lunch in preference to shooting straight through.

After lunch, we normally do a single big drive, but today we do two so as to try something untried. We are honoured to be the guinea pigs for Cwm Copper, a drive not used at Stanage for some years. The wind is tricky and the birds come out of the hilly scrub were not expected – Jonathan shifts the line, moves the guns, and curses most eloquently (NB eloquence in cursing consists of sixteen-letter words that are creative combinations of four-letter standards, with some local colour added; steadiness of intent, steadfastness of content and breath control are as important to this form of cursing as vocabulary, and Jonathan is a master). However, belying his skilful descriptives, all Guns get good shooting, mostly at partridge, which have taken the fierce and arbitrary wind and made it their own. As many effectless shots are fired, there is a bit of mumbling on the line that also might be vulgar language, but the heavy lunch has suppressed everyone's volume, so I cannot be certain.

We have shot reasonably well today, I later find, having averaged about 4.6 cartridges fired for each bird killed. At Stanage, that is a respectable performance.

Then, exhilarated from the pleasures of Cwm Copper, back to the house for tea (with delicate tea sandwiches, cakes, scones and clotted cream) as it has again been almost two hours since we were last fed. There is time for a nap or a few surreptitious phone calls (many in the group are active business people, but no one wants to be seen being active in these surroundings, harking to the rhythm of an earlier era of 'trade is not for gentlemen'). Then cocktails and dinner. More glorious food (and wine). More glorious conversation. More humour (none involving *ovis aries*). Bed. The rooms are all wonderfully comfortable, charmingly furbished.

The second day should proceed mechanically like the first, but at the draw for pegs, I cheat and select the marker for the peg next to my most fearsome poacher, to whom, I know, it will bring a special pleasure. The other fearsome poacher cheats to get the peg on my other side. Competitive juices are all aflow. The other Guns, good friends and polite people, shake their heads at our breach of shooting courtesy, but do not intervene.

The second, third and fourth drives of this day are the ones that will turn out to give us the greatest scope for childlike glee and we relish it. Birds at each drive are exquisitely shown along the entire line, birds so perfect that our faces start to look like a contagion of rictus has swept in on the swift Welsh winds.

The second drive is called Holloway Oak. The tallest hill on the Welsh side of the property lowers over a valley studded with small ponds. Wind descends from somewhere fierce, the Arctic perhaps, or Mars, and sends pheasant so high and so fast that our ratio of cartridges fired to birds killed goes well into double digits. It is perhaps the most beautiful of drives to watch when the light is right, as it is today. No one shoots well – Jonathan and the inestimable Dylan Williams of the Royal Berkshire Shooting School are standing behind me, chortling, loud enough to be sure I can hear. Dylan achieved a MacNab last season and has been chortling at flawed mortals ever since. We are beyond the limits of our skills, but there are nonetheless birds killed, and each is a lifetime memory because each is splendid. Each such bird, and there are not many, gets an exclamation of admiration from all who see its downfall. Only perfect shots are successful here; Jonathan tells me that some of the greatest shots in England (remember, he is one) have left this drive in a combination of admiration and frustration. The birds are exquisitely shown and are, for the best Guns, at the very tip of range – no slight deviation from perfect will bring down any of these birds. We are not the best Guns in England and enjoy the opportunity to display our failings. We leave behind a large population of birds which no longer fears guns. Bravo, pheasants!

The third drive, Middle Pits, is again in a valley, but here we are deep in the woods with Guns standing along the banks of a swift stream. For some it is the prettiest setting of all – the view corridor is from twenty to fifty yards up or down stream and perhaps twenty yards straight across, then straight up a wooded slope to old growth forest. The birds fly past over the trees topping the banks. I do not know how high this is, but it is very high, and the time from when you see a bird to when you do not is very short. I finally have a drive at which I shoot beyond my skill level, cannot miss, and am enthused enough to take a few shots that are beyond my range, but far enough in front that the whole shot-string must hit the bird to kill it. Two cock birds that would have given superb opportunities to my brilliant nemeses on either side are dispatched this way to reluctant applause, even, in one case, a distinct whoop of respect. The setting in the trees, on the stream, with friends in either direction and testing birds perfectly presented, this is much how I imagine shooting will be in heaven (unless, of course, heaven is operated by pheasants).

Lunch again, splendid and excessive again, then The Knoll. I am pleased to have a back gun behind me on this very traditional drive near the Castle, as I am shooting poorly (it must be the fault of the lovely Boss side-levers I am shooting, since I have proven my formidable ability on the previous drive). The birds, pheasant and partridge, are driven from woods well in front of us above a long slope, then fly to high woods close behind us – these birds tower in a few wing beats, set wings and ride the jet stream (ok, the wind) well over our heads and at varied angles. As the drive progresses, the keeper has decided that we have shot enough of his birds, and at the very end of the drive, he pushes great flights of many birds over all at once, so we cannot possibly kill many. It is an opulent display, a glory of pheasant indeed, and a wonderful finish to the day's shooting.

In sum, there is no 'ordinary' drive at Stanage. Each shares the qualities of challenging birds, exquisite landscape, and excellent professional presentation.

Great praise is well earned for the keepers and beaters who are able to produce such quality – this has been a difficult year for presentation of birds in the region. Winds have been shifty, or from the wrong direction or not extant at all when needed. Birds have struggled with excessively wet, dry, cold and hot weather, each extreme arriving when least desired. Standing in a line of Guns it is easy to forget the professionals who accomplish the miracles. Their very invisibility most of the time is a sign of their professionalism. And, the pickers-up at Stanage have another most difficult job. They must often work hundreds of yards behind the guns to find birds that drop at long distances, coast on high winds down long slopes or are, alas, pricked rather than killed. The pickers miss very few and give us a great display of dog work in the process.

On the lists of the great sporting shoots of England, Stanage is ubiquitous. But a truly great shoot experience engages the heart, the head, the eye as well as the sport. Our hearts sing with the friendship of special people, our heads are filled with the exquisite planning and professional execution, our eyes are served brilliantly by the landscape of the estate and the wonderful interiors of Stanage, and, the sport itself cannot be shown better.

It is a cold, wet, grey morning in New York as I write this, and the writing brings longing for those variegated joys.

Favourite Shoots
Richard Purdey

Arkleside Moor, Middleham, North Yorkshire

It was Martin Vallance who generously gave me my first taste of grouse shooting in September 1999, four years after he'd embarked on his superb restoration of Arkleside Moor, above Coverdale, North Yorkshire. When Martin acquired Arkleside in 1995 the moor was effectively barren, over grazed, the heather in a bad way, with few grouse and little biodiversity. By 1999 the grouse were back, starting to reward his patience, efforts and investment.

Being my first experience of grouse, and double guns, Arkleside remains forever one of the most unforgettable days in my shooting career, every drive still clearly etched in my memory. Martin assigned me to Bob, a loader with over fifty seasons of grouse shooting under his belt. His kindly advice and calming presence were invaluable to a nervous novice, and reassuring too for host and fellow Guns!

Having drawn number four, we recovered our breath after the long climb to the butt and waited for the first drive to start. 'Aye, there they are,' Bob said quietly, 'over there look.' Across the vast undulating expanse of heather, a thousand yards out, we caught our first glimpse of the advancing line of beaters. Occasionally, tantalizingly, a covey of grouse would get up, only to drop back in to the heather, but each time a couple of hundred yards or so nearer.

Two shots suddenly rang out, from what sounded like number one. 'They'll be on us any second' said Bob, then more urgently, 'Now Sir, now, coming in from ten o'clock.' The shooting school instructor's words flashed up. 'Shoot 'em well out in front and knock their socks off!' It was easy with clays! This was quite different. I brought the gun up to a fast low grouse following the contour line. Damn! Missed the blighter. I could see exactly how too, from the white mist where the shot had torn into the dew laden heather. Just behind. We swapped guns. 'On your right Sir', and sweeping in from two o'clock, came four more. I fired at the first and, unforgettably, it fell dead into the heather twenty-five yards in front of the butt. My second barrel missed. I changed guns again, remembering to turn round before mounting the gun, and fired at the fourth and last bird. It dropped like a stone, straight into a gully fifty yards behind the butt. I'd done it; my first brace of grouse. Two further shots went unrewarded, and in my elation I never even saw, until far too late, the three birds that appeared without warning from behind that protruding knoll above and to our right. And in that vein the day continued, with three more drives and a grouse on each before lunch, and afterwards two more drives and another brace and a half before the final horn sounded. The bag for the day was forty-six and a half brace.

We drove home that evening, weary but exhilarated, reflecting that it's not just the challenge and adrenaline rush that makes shooting these marvellous fast flying wild birds the most coveted of all shooting invitations, but the whole unique experience of being up on the moors, the wind, the smells, the big skies, the oceans of heather, the secret gullies and tumbling ghylls, and, not least, trying to do justice to all that hard work that the owner, the keeper, the under-keepers and the beaters all put in to get those grouse over the Guns. Nothing else quite compares.

Brightling Park, near Battle, East Sussex

Far closer to home, deep in East Sussex, and less than ten miles from Senlac Hill where King Harold fell in 1066, lies the beautiful Brightling Park estate, owned by the Grissell family. The Park is home to the Brightling Horse Trials and to the Brightling Park Shoot, the latter being run by Henry Grissell. The estate covers several hundred acres of unspoiled hilly Wealden countryside, a lovely combination of woodland and open fields, offering excellent pheasant shooting from November onwards. Brightling doesn't have the topography to present stratospherically high birds, but on breezy days the top drives challenge even the best of shots.

One of Brightling's charms is that since 'Elf and Safety' and EU regulations combined to stop Henry using his old 'Gun Bus', once the back half of a five-ton lorry with a row of tip-up red velvet cinema seats one side and an old church pew the other, towed by Henry on his tractor, the Guns now walk from drive to drive. This is a far better way to appreciate the lie of the land and how the shoot works. Whilst fine for fitter Guns, and for building a healthy appetite for lunch, it's no good for the halt or the lame; Brightling's clay is infamous. But fear not: Henry ensures that anyone who cannot manage the walking can hitch a ride on the quad bike, which is also the transport for everyone's guns and shells – and, equally importantly, the refreshments.

Local bangers and a 'slogasm' (sloe gin and champagne) are customarily served after the second drive. After the fourth, lunch in the 'pavilion' is a further highpoint. The pavilion is in fact a small tiled roof stone building looking across Brightling's hallowed cricket ground, more potting shed than pavilion, but which doubles in summer as the village cricket team's HQ. Within presides Henry's wife Helena, producing amazing roasts from an ancient gas cooker, while the Guns sit round the long scrubbed table, warmed by a roaring log fire. After a great morning's shooting, this is heaven, a proper shoot lunch before the final drive or two of the afternoon.

Lees Court, near Faversham, Kent

Some thirty miles or so to the north-east of Brightling lies the village of Charing, once a busy staging post on the A20, the old Kent road from London to the channel ports. Charing sits snugly under the North Downs, the magnificent rolling chalk countryside terminating abruptly to the east in the white cliffs of Dover – and re-emerging eastward through the Pas de Calais. This is a land of well drained flinty soil, dry valleys, steep escarpments, and hanging woods: prime partridge country.

Lying in the folds of the North Downs between Charing and the historic old town of Faversham is a compact and well run estate shooting over some 700 acres: Lees Court. The big house was sold in the 1970s to become retirement flats, but the name also lives on for the shoot, whose HQ is a charming and superbly restored farmhouse close to the village of Shottenden. Shooting parties are royally looked after by the butler George, and his highly professional catering team, in a superbly converted barn alongside the house. Let days at Lees Court are frequently hosted personally by Lees Court Estate's charming American owner, Lady Sondes. Her late husband, Lord Sondes, who died in the mid 1990s, was a fanatical Shot, and took infinite pains in developing the shoot's rich variety of drives with his headkeeper John Fountain. John is still very much in charge of the keepering and his brother Julian leads the dedicated team of beaters. The Fountain brothers are the third generation to work on the estate. Ken, a county ploughing champion and the home farm's tractor driver, looks after the Guns' trailer, while the game cart is under the eagle eye of the wonderfully lugubrious Richard, who keeps the tally of shots fired and birds picked up on a blackboard. These characters are real countrymen, blessed with wicked senses of humour and rich lines in repartee. They know the shoot backwards, in all its moods, understand the birds, how the weather and the wind will affect different drives and how and where the birds fly. These loyal staff and family links imbue Lees Court with a very special atmosphere and charm, and guests are made to feel so welcome they quickly feel at home.

As you would expect in this terrain, many of Lees Court's drives are predominantly partridge. These drives are capable of putting excellent birds over the Guns, but need to be blanked in from quite long distances, so it can take time before they show. But the Frenchmen fly well here and are worth the wait.

There are also several first-class pheasant drives from either side of the woods, which flank the estate's principal, and long, dry valley. Don't expect huge numbers or out of range high birds, but a steady flow of excitingly challenging pheasant, with the odd partridge joining in the fun, will keep the whole line on their toes.

The Cream of Northern England
Jose Pepe Fanjul

Gunnerside

I have known Gunnerside for many years having been invited to shoot in the past by friends who used to take it from the previous owner, but I was never able to go. I have now gone for several years as the guest of my friend, Bob Miller, the current owner, who has made an undeniably important mark on the shoot, the Lodge and the area in general. Bob Miller is not only a great shot, a gracious host, but also a very nice guy who enjoys every aspect of his estate and knows it like the palm of his hand. There is no better or more complete grouse moor than Gunnerside. You can shoot six beats straight without ever repeating the same ground and always be in beautiful surroundings with great shooting. I don't know of another moor that can shoot six straight days of that quality anywhere.

The moor is kept to perfection with great tender loving care down to every detail. The Lodge is very comfortable, the food delicious and the company always great. What a combination! I always remember waking up in the morning and looking at the grouse moor out my window, one of the prettiest sights one could have anywhere; just the right ingredients to whet your appetite for the rest of the day. Again, this is purely a private shoot and is run as such by someone who appreciates and loves every aspect of the sport and is lethal with his 20-bore guns.

Wemmergill

The first time I shot at Wemmergill, I was the guest of Joe Nickerson in the 1970s who at the time had a long lease on the shoot and made many improvements. It is funny how I first went there as I got a call from Joe who I did not know at the time, but he had heard of me as we had many friends in common so he very kindly invited me to come stay and shoot. I accepted with pleasure, but did not go and stay as I had my whole family plus my dog with me, which I thought was a bit much, so I stayed at a hotel nearby and went to shoot. After that year, we all returned, stayed and shot with him every year until he died.

Shooting grouse with Joe Nickerson at Wemmergill was not only a pleasure, but an education. He was at the time the most knowledgeable person on grouse shooting, had studied everything about grouse and was in my view the best grouse Shot of his era. He was a controversial character. You either loved him or you didn't. To me and my family, he was only kind, generous and nice so I was in the category of those who loved him and to this day, I miss him.

The shooting day at Wemmergill with Joe started always with a picture taken in front of the house with the shooting party and then everybody went to the shoot with their own vehicle with one's loader and gear, which made it extremely comfortable as you had everything in hand. Joe would always carry a small dictating machine in his case where he would dictate all his comments on the day's shooting, which were typed by a secretary at the end of the day and given to the headkeeper for future reference. He was a true perfectionist and the combination of this love and knowledge of grouse shooting was unsurpassed. Some of the drives were unique and very historical. I remember having some of my most memorable days there. Joe always had a double line of beaters at Wemmergill so we would always shoot six drives with very little wait in between drives so it was never a long day. Lunch was always delicious and just the right amount of time was spent lunching, as with Joe there was never any time wasted.

I had the privilege of shooting at the Kaiser's but a few times, which was quite amusing as apparently he had a hidden spot behind his butt where he would have an assistant shoot the birds he would miss to make him look good in front of the other Guns. It is so ridiculous that it is quite funny if you think about it!

Alnwick

I met the present Duke of Northumberland, then Lord Ralph Percy, grouse shooting in the Lammermuirs when he was buying Burncastle for the Northumberland Estates and at the time, he very kindly invited me to shoot at Alnwick where I have now been shooting for approximately fifteen years. I can tell you that Alnwick was always a good shoot, but it continues to improve every season. I don't think there is a pheasant shoot anywhere better kept or managed with more tender loving care than Alnwick. I know that the shoot along with the Castle are the pride and joy of both the Duke and Duchess and justifiably so. They have beautifully redone and restored the entire Castle to absolute perfection in superb taste and comfort. From the moment you arrive, you can feel the love they have for the Estate and their home. There is no more comfortable or beautiful place to stay and shoot pheasants than Alnwick. It is a step back in time, but with modern comforts. In addition to that, Jane, the present Duchess, has created Alnwick Gardens, which has become one of the most famous and popular destinations in the north of England and a world famous garden by any standards. The shoot itself has changed and continues to improve. The easier drives are no longer used and new spectacular high pheasant drives have been created to complement the high ones they already had. I especially like to shoot both sides of the bunkers and a new drive they have created on a ridge on the side of a hill. In these three drives, you will find as high and as difficult pheasants as you will in any place in the UK.

While I give this combination pheasant shoot and Castle a ten out of ten and would tempt anybody to call and contact Alnwick with a view to taking a pheasant shoot, unfortunately, I must tell you that it is not available as it is purely a family shoot and they have no interest in letting it. There is nothing commercial about the shoot and it is run purely for their pleasure. I feel privileged that I am afforded one of the two weekends a year that they let to friends.

Shooting with Ralph at Northumberland is also a remarkable experience whether it is grouse, pheasant or partridge. He is without a doubt one of the best all around Guns alive today and his love of shooting and country sports in general is legend. The Northumberlands are truly happy people living and enjoying the paradise they have, while at the same time giving back by helping create opportunities for the people of the area.

Miltons
Majid Jafar

I have had the pleasure and the privilege of international variety in my shooting career – whether Hungarian pheasants, Scottish grouse, Argentinean doves, Spanish partridge, or South African francolin and guinea fowl; each game bird combined with the special terrain and local shooting traditions brings a unique and memorable experience to be treasured.

There is nonetheless something special about driven pheasant and partridge shooting in the UK, and of all the areas in the UK, the valleys of Devon hold a special place in my heart. There are many excellent shoots in the West Country, all famous for presenting high and challenging birds. I have been lucky to have shot at several of them, including Molland, West Molland, Chargot, Clovelly, and Haddeo. My favourite shoot of all however is undoubtedly Miltons.

Situated around the village of Bridgetown, to the north of Dulverton on Exmoor, the Miltons Shoot led the way when the Great Shoots of Exmoor were pioneered in the early 1980s, and since then, the shoot has continued to develop the stunning ground to realize its full potential. A relatively compact 5,000 acres, the very best of the dramatic topography has led to the development of famous pheasant drives such as Collies Head, Howe Wood, Tom's Hedges, Rookery and Dark Corner. My personal favourite is Howe Wood (re-named 'Helm's Deep' by a friend of mine, after the battle scene in the Lord of the Rings film series!), where a steady stream of high and beautifully presented birds continued to fly evenly over the whole shooting line of nine Guns. A close second would be Tom's Hedges, which can be outstanding in the right wind.

Aside from the pheasants, the partridges at Miltons have a loyal following too, with old established drives such as Farm, Church, Squeakitts-Top and Aerial all providing excellent sport. I have shot there on all-partridge days in September and October, but my favourite days would be the mixed days in mid November, when both pheasant and partridge drives can be combined to make truly special days of sport.

In the middle of the estate is Hollam Farm, where lunch and tea are provided with lots of the delicious local produce – beef, clotted cream, cheddar and all the other goodies the West Country is known for, as well as local ales and good wines.

Headkeeper Paul Lugg (fondly known as 'Luggie') runs a very organized but friendly team, and indeed what truly makes Miltons special for me is the relaxed and welcoming atmosphere that in a subtle yet important way differentiates it from the other big commercial shoots. They may shoot several days a week, yet you never *feel* that when you are there – from the smiles of the beaters to the relaxed pace of the day and the attention to detail, there is no sense that you are there just to shoot birds, but rather to enjoy the day with all that it should entail. A host is really made to feel like the host, and a guest is really made to feel like a guest. Apart from the truly special birds and the uniquely beautiful terrain, that's what really sets Miltons apart.

Ireland

I have been a very fortunate man and have hunted and fished from Alaska to Zambia. But as I grew older my burning passion, indeed addiction, for big game hunting waned. In its place I found my old love of bird shooting stronger than ever. And of all the bird shooting possibilities my preference has always leaned towards driven game. In 1997, I moved to Ireland in order to pursue this pastime to its fullest. Why Ireland and not England? Simple, my girlfriend owned a shoot in Ireland.

The ecology and environment in Ireland is diverse, but changing. The extreme west, especially Galway, Mayo and some other counties, are extremely bleak with as much stone in the ground as loam. Wicklow, the midlands and the south-east tend to be extremely lush and green. While there are significant areas of heather it is over grazed by sheep and, therefore, does not provide suitable habitat to support more than the occasional grouse. Much of the old hardwoods were deforested long ago and a large government/private service called Coillte has aggressively reforested the countryside. The down side is that some wonderful bog land that produced good snipe shooting has been drained and forested. That said, large bogs and good sport still exist.

While there are thousands of shoots in the UK, driven shooting in Ireland is restricted to a mere handful of shoots, most of which are located in County Wicklow. These are Ballyarthur, Ballinacor, Castle Howard, Coolattin, Glendalough, Shelton Abbey and Shillelagh. The other Irish shoots of interest to the foreign sportsman are Crooked Wood, Dromoland and the Nire Valley. Of the previous list Ballyarthur, Castle Howard, Glendalough and Shelton Abbey are primarily syndicate shoots that each let out three to four commercial days to pump up their revenues. There are perhaps another dozen shoots in the country that are strictly syndicate.

Driven Pheasant and Duck

Ballinacor

Established over thirty years ago, Ballinacor has become the shoot in Ireland against which all other shoots must be judged. A small shoot at first, it has grown into a very serious shoot with over 30,000 pheasants put down on 4,000 acres of land. The terrain and topography coupled with a terrific headkeeper, Keith Wooldridge, who was trained at Broadlands (Lord Mountbatten's shoot in England), combined to produce drive after drive of very good quality, though not on a par with the top British shoots. There are a few commercial days, most of which are always sold well in advance.

Ballinacor changed hands about five years ago. Sir Robert and Lady Goff are committed to continuing the great sport at Ballinacor. I shot Ballinacor once or twice a year as guests of syndicate members. The final two times, Sir Robert apologized to me for the days not going better. Perhaps they were shooting it too much. At Ballinacor one has the option of shooting single days of about 300 birds, or for those with very deep pockets, double days with double guns and no bag limit. While they do have a few four to five star drives, I have never been on a day with more than one or two of those drives offered. Our friend, the late, great Dr Tony Ryan (Ryanair), told me the year before he died that his team shot almost 700 birds. Unfortunately, his team, no offence, could not manage that on any top shoot in the West Country, Scotland or Wales

Castle Howard

Castle Howard, owned by Ivor Fitzpatrick, one of Ireland's leading solicitors, produces outstanding shooting (two spectacular, two very good drives on a typical day), on land that is blessed with the topography necessary to accomplish this one or two days a week. Six seasons ago they acquired additional farms that produce some spectacular shooting indeed. The new land is basically a long ravine divided by a rail track and river where birds can be flown from one side to the other with the Guns in the middle. Bags tend to hover in the region of 400 birds. In eleven seasons, I have seen this shoot grow from a small private shoot, to one of significant proportions.

The best shoot in the Ireland.

Shillelagh

Owned by Humewood Castle, it had quickly established itself as a shoot with which to be reckoned. The biggest problem with Shillelagh was that many drives were too good. No Irish shoot produced taller birds. A largish number of drives allowed them to tailor the day to suit the team and it was one of the five best shoots in the country. The *Shooting Times*, on 27 January 2000, made it a cover story and gave it five stars, a tad generous, but we had a good day. (Sadly, we closed this shoot. While the birds were sky high we were too easy to poach, our keepers were less than brilliant, and the returns were too low.)

Humewood

Humewood was renowned as a duck shoot of significant proportions. Four lakes provided five drives and most seasons saw a few big bag (500+) days. The main limitations as to the size of the bag (250–400 mallard were typical) were the quality of the shooting and the depths of the pockets. The birds fly spectacularly and as pointed out in the April 1999 Bird Hunting Report newsletter 'described by many as the best flighted duck in the British Isles'.

As Bill Montgomery, who owns his own private shoot in the UK and represents Sotheby's in Ireland, said 'this is duck shooting for the cognoscenti'. Very elegant lunches and very grand overall is why the *Condé Nast Traveller* called Humewood 'One of the fifty greatest private villas in the world'. Humewood prided itself on providing grand, Edwardian-style house parties.

We recently sold the Castle. Hopefully the new owners will reinstate the duck shoot.

Glendalough

Glendalough is a large property on the east side of County Wicklow. Run as a commercial and syndicate shoot by the owner until a decade ago, it is now completely in the hands of the syndicate. They have improved a previously very good shoot dramatically. Their keeper is very good and the land lends itself to presenting very good birds. They sell a few commercial days. Harry Harrison and Paul Cran who run the syndicate and the shoot are charming, urbane individuals. It is one of the five or six best shoots in Ireland.

Crooked Wood

Crooked Wood is a very large shoot in terms of acreage, four or five thousand acres on the shores of Loch Derravara. Frank Gibson, who owns most of the land and leases the rest, runs a very fine shoot. He is expanding to a larger operation shooting more days and bigger bags for next season. Frank is a first-rate man and operator and three of his drives produce spectacularly tall birds. Guests are housed at Crooked Wood House (no affiliation), which is a very nice hotel with very good food.

Coolattin

Coolattin estate was once one of the largest properties in Ireland – of many thousands of acres. Since its heyday it has been broken up into many separate properties, which now include a golf course, the separate Shillelagh shoot (q.v.), various farms and woodland properties. The terrain lends itself to showing good birds and they shoot at least two days a week in November and December with an occasional third day added. In the 1999 season, I would have rated it highly. In 2000 there were too many immature, very late birds coming out of the drives – positively unseemly. Until mid December they looked like poults. Sixty-eight shoot days did not help. Typical commercial days provide bags of 300–350 birds. In 2001, shoot days dropped to fifty-eight, but significant numbers of late birds were still evident. I shot there eight days in 2000, two days in 2001. The occasional red leg partridge and duck come through the drives as well. The shooting improved in the last few seasons. It is a good shoot for the average to good shot.

Dromoland

I have shot at Dromoland a few times in the last ten years but only once on a driven day. This unusual shoot shoots nearly every day for the first four to six weeks of the season and then almost calls it quits to driven days and switches to rough shooting and 'mini drives' for smaller groups of Guns and dramatically smaller bags. The quality of the pheasant at Dromoland from my limited experience is good without ever approaching greatness. What is particularly surprising is that there are almost no birds in a drive that one will let go because they are too low but, most unfortunately, almost no birds that are memorable either. (I killed fifty-two birds with fifty-seven cartridges, some shot twice. These were sporting birds, not archangels, in the thirty-five-plus yard range and I was having a good day. This would not have been possible at Castle Howard, Ballinacor or Shillelagh.) Woodcock occasionally come through on the drives.

Shelton Abbey

The property is now owned by the government as a low-security facility for white-collar criminals and the shooting rights are leased. I needed some additional days for clients and viewed the shoot. It shot reasonably well, probably the best day there that I experienced. Birds were in the thirty to thirty-five-yard range, coming off a long cliff face on which they have four drives.

I took one team there and it shot well enough. I shot it another day, their 'Christmas shoot', as a guest of a syndicate member and it had a dreadful partridge drive, quite a good drive on a different side of the shoot, and two others that I cannot recall. Then I took another team and booked it for a day midweek. The day did not go well. It started with a weird drive near the gates of the prison where delivery trucks nearly ran over dogs. That was followed with one of the drives on the cliff face. Unfortunately, few birds went over the line – another unmemorable drive followed by their better drive on the other side mentioned above.

The bag was not met and enough cartridges were not fired. I was not pleased. On speaking to the syndicate captain, he said we should have booked a weekend as they could not get enough beaters and pickers. If I had been told before, I would have had the team shoot Coolattin that day and Shelton on the weekend as I had the ability to choose dates. Coolattin, being more professionally organized, can get beaters midweek.

If only the guy had mentioned his qualms any time before the day, these problems need not have arisen. Such was life in County Wicklow.

Woodcock

Ireland's driven woodcock shooting was legendary. Ashford Castle and many of the stately homes were originally designed around driven woodcock shooting. Today there are only a handful of estates that cater purely for woodcock shooters. Woodcock require warm woods on cold days. Prior to the large reforestation of Ireland those few shoots that planted large woodlands especially for woodcock shooting would attract the birds like magnets from the bleak moorland or peat bogs that surrounded them. Today, more land is suitable for woodcock and therefore they are not as concentrated as they were as recently as 1950 when tremendous driven shoots could be had at Glenstal Abbey in County Limerick, Lissadell in county Sligo and the most famous of all, Ashford Castle in County Galway.

The best woodcock shooting I have ever had was in the Outer Hebrides of Scotland at Garynahine, owned at the time by a syndicate of Americans. One day I killed nine birds to my own gun and seven the next.

Humewood Castle, before they bought the Shillelagh shoot, had a small property called Kilmurray on the eastern edge of County Wicklow overlooking the Irish Sea, where as many as nineteen woodcock had been pushed out of a single pheasant drive. Frank Maunsell, one of the best professional dog handlers, had a stellar walk-up season a few years ago with 248 birds to his own gun in County Kerry. It was, as he put it, the best season of the decade. Which brings me to the second most important point of woodcock shooting; being completely wild, and of a migratory nature, there are good years and bad, and good days and bad. One can control as many details as possible but there is always an element of chance, which determines the quality of sport. That said, the most important element to driven woodcock shooting is safety. Woodcock, while always offering an interesting target, frequently present an unsafe one. A low bird taken in front can mean a beater's eye. Care must be taken not to shoot through the line as grave consequences can result.

Cong

The land of the great Ashford shoot was leased by Michael Ryan who controlled 35,000 acres in the area for woodcock and snipe shooting. If you hit it right, dry and cold, the shooting can be spectacular. The day I shot there the conditions were wrong, windy and wet and still everyone had opportunities to kill woodcock and birds were shot on eleven of twelve drives. It is a very interesting experience and reasonably priced. Michael Ryan was a knowledgeable, reputable, and charming operator/host. One has two choices of hotels in the town of Cong. The first is Ryan's bed and breakfast, which is a small hotel with very small bedrooms, located in the centre of town. Most shooters appreciate it for the *craic* (the Irish term for good sport, fun and laughs). The other is Ashford Castle, which is a five-star deluxe hotel. I have stayed there on two or three occasions, once with a nice but ordinary room, but this last time a spectacular suite. Michael Ryan recently passed away but I understand that his brother still runs the shoot from Ryan's bed and breakfast.

Snipe

There are two types of bogs that attract snipe. The first is known as 'green' or 'black'. This type is marshy, swampy land. Of more interest to the shooter are the raised 'heathery' bogs known as 'red' bogs as they produce the best shooting. The birds tend to concentrate on them as the full moon approaches. While snipe inhabit the large wet marshy 'black' bogs they are difficult to find as they are highly dispersed on them.

Gun Licences

Gun licence application forms must be provided by the operator and completed by the tourist/sportsman. For non EU citizens, a current hunting licence/ firearms permit/good conduct letter from the police or letter of membership to a shooting club must be attached. If your country is a member of the EU, you must send your *original EU Firearm pass* (not a Xerox) with the application and payment. If the form is completed accurately, two to four weeks are necessary to process. Six weeks allows sufficient time in case required information is omitted. One flies to Shannon to shoot woodcock in Cong or Dromoland and for some of the rough shoots mentioned. Dublin is the airport for the majority of the shoots and most are within an hour to an hour and a half of the airport.

Part III – Scandinavia

Denmark

(Note: This is based on ten days' shooting in the mid to late 1980s and is out of date, though the shooting is much the same now.)

The arrival of the noble pheasant in Denmark is a relatively recent event, much more recent than the introduction of the species in other parts of Western Europe.

Kragerupgard (*gard* means estate or farm) belongs to the Dinesen family. Eric Dinesen's title, Master of the Royal Hunt, ranks between baron and count. He is a cousin of Isak Dinesen, the Baroness Blixen whose writings on the veldt of Africa are classic. The nobility of Denmark, like that of so much of the world, largely comprises sportsmen. So it is not surprising that Dinesen, like his famous cousin before him, shoots. What is impressive is that both he and his brother were considered two of Denmark's top four or five shooters.

Dinesen rarely shoots now, but rather leased the shooting rights to Dr Liland. Economic realities, the huge Danish income tax and a wealth tax forces this on many estates. In the old days, nobility managed the shoots exclusively for its own pleasure, but having foreign sportsmen in is better than the alternative. Estates can manage to remain intact and a large staff of gamekeepers can be maintained. The alternative is selling off to create smaller parcels and that would be a travesty for both the men and for the game.

The first drive at Kragerupgard was through a fairly dense forest with the shooters positioned along the road. The birds were pushed high overhead. These were strong flying birds, tall birds as the English would say, though not nearly so tall as the best British shoots, and the wind helped much. One had hardly any warning, only the noisy beating of their wings. The first bird got by me before I could even raise my gun. The next few were missed as I adjusted to the lead required, got the kinks out from jet lag and went to work.

In the second drive, Prince Moritz Oettingen-Wallenstein, who lived in New York at the time and is a friend, and I shot behind the line on clean-up duty. The shooters directly in front of us were so good that we got relatively little sport. But what we did get was classic, the birds again flying very well.

On the third drive, the last before lunch, half the line walked behind the beaters to shoot turning birds. They had great fun. The other half of the line stood in an open valley below. Never have I seen such a pheasant shoot outside of England. The wind was truly howling and the birds zigged and zagged just like doves. It was a unique experience. They flew amazingly well and the majority of the birds escaped.

Running a drive to produce good sport is an art. The terrain, cover and trees must be just right to hold the birds and drive them to fly up high. The gamekeeper must understand how to drive. In Denmark, he steers his line of beaters with a horn to signal a change in direction or to stop and start at appropriate times. If there is too much noise the birds will run too fast and too far. When they do finally go up, they do so in a huge group, a bouquet of a hundred or more birds. While it is a magnificent spectacle to watch, it provides very little sport; by the time one has fired off a few shots, they are gone and most of the line has had no opportunity to shoot.

In the good old days of Denmark, children were given the day off from school to participate in the drives. Today, dogs augment the efforts of the beaters and, by quartering in a controlled manner, they help put up birds in generally manageable numbers. In the four days of shooting I witnessed only three mass flushes or bouquets; one against a backdrop of the Baltic Sea, one with the North Sea as a background and one while beating a patch surrounded by fields.

Actually, much of the day staff, especially the dog handlers, work without pay. Frequently they are themselves gamekeepers at other estates and lend their services, expecting and receiving like help when their lease is being shot. Others are simply dog owners who welcome the opportunity to work their animals. They are also able to participate in the shoots put on for them at the end of the season.

Lechenborg was to be the fifth and final estate to be shot. We had already experienced two very good days and one good day of pheasant hunting plus a day on raised mallards flighted off ponds.

The day ends with speeches and words of thanks from the landowner and Dr

Liland. A game count follows. Then the horn blowers – one to four in our shoots – go to work. The birds are laid out in a descending pecking order, starting with the woodcock, then cock pheasant, hen pheasant, ducks and finally wood pigeon. The marches are blown for each species in order, followed by taps. On especially festive occasions, the Hubertus march is blown first, St Hubertus being the patron saint of hunters.

How does Denmark compare with England? That is a difficult question and I raise it because I'm certain many readers have wondered about this. The very best of England is unrivalled. Denmark's shoots provide birds in excellent numbers, even allowing for the larger lines, and they are generally of good but not great sporting standard. Five hundred to six hundred bird days are the norm, though larger bags can be booked with much advance notice by the party. An occasional woodcock is often seen. The land is much less severe than in England, so there are not so many hillsides overlooking ravines that provide the ultimate pheasant shooting challenge.

Dr Liland is a charming, educated man. He has over thirty years' experience in organizing the top shooting in Denmark. He has moved his base of operation to Sorup Estate near Ringsted, a location that offers a number of advantages, as I quickly learned during my most recent trip to the estate. First, it is more centrally located, reducing driving time most days. It also has an enormous house with a very large indoor swimming pool and sauna, and should provide an outstanding home for the week. He also provides incredible accommodation and food.

On the third day, half a day's duck shooting is provided, followed by a half day in Copenhagen. Sorup Manor is centrally located and close to all the shooting, so changing hotels is not necessary and a minimum of time is lost travelling to the estates hunted.

Dress code is less formal that in England. Duck shoots are offered in September and October. Ten Guns can expect to shoot 400 to 600 birds a day.

Guns of 12 gauge certainly are an advantage on pheasant and duck, but one would not be dramatically handicapped with a 20-gauge. Birds tend to be medium height, so stay away from excessive choking.

Part IV – Eastern Europe

The shoots of Eastern Europe promise a lot and deliver somewhat less. Many people are drawn to these shoots because with a per bird price in the mid-20s (Euro) they seem appealing. The truth is that the bags tend to be very big, often 600 or more birds a day, and many of the shoots have hidden extra costs, either in terms of gun or hunting licences, insurance and sometimes transport. When one adds all these prices together, one could have experienced a first-class 300 bird British day and have fired more cartridges. Some writers claim that the shoots of Eastern Europe are as good as the best British shoots. This is not true. In fact, what this really tells me is that the writers have not been to the top British shoots, such as Castle Hill or Whitfield.

This is not to say that these shoots are not right for some shooters. If you want a big bag shooting low to medium birds, depending on estate, drives and conditions, then these shoots are fine. These are also great shoots for 28-gauge guns.

Occasionally, tall drives are presented.

Slovakia

I shot for three days in Slovakia a few seasons ago and must say that the birds here, I felt, are as good as or better than Hungary or the Czech Republic. Unlike some of the estates/forests in Hungary, all of these birds seem to be driven. The problem was that on some of the estates they really did not fully grasp the concept of driving pheasants. On some of the drives the birds would drop into the woods just in front of the team of Guns. Guns were pegged too close to the woods. They would then drive them a second time but the birds were too close to the Guns to gain altitude or speed, in part being tired from their first flight. (A pheasant is like a sprinter not a marathon runner. He can only flap his wings for seven or eight seconds – that does not include glide time – and then like a sprinter who has given his all in a hundred-yard dash, he is exhausted.) Because of this inability to continue to fly, reverse drives do not work well unless the birds are rested for about an hour, for example while the team has lunch.

My group stayed at Chateau Vozokany, about an hour from Bratislava, which is a large manor house with four excellent big bedrooms and so-so food. The operator who I work with did an excellent job of supplying caviar, proper stuff from Russia, and champagne, improper stuff also from Russia. It is my understanding that Vozokany is in need of refurbishing at this point and that Habsburg Castle is the best place to stay. Another advantage of Slovakia is that they will accept teams as small as four for Chateau Vozokany and also shoot smaller bags.

The Czech Republic

Konopiste

I have shot the Czech Republic a couple of times with different groups. Konopiste, about an hour outside of Prague, is considered by many to be the best shoot in Eastern Europe. Christian Zoske is a very well spoken multilingual German who basically inherited this shoot from his father. It is situated in the grounds of the Royal Castle of Archduke Ferdinand.

Unfortunately, it is expensive by Eastern European standards at about 30 Euros a bird. Additionally, is has those extra costs both for licences and transport, and they really want to shoot a minimum of 600 birds, so they tend to give, or at least prefer giving, three or four mediocre drives before lunch to make the bag easily and only offer the good drives in the ravine afterwards. Some of the teams feel that they are so far into overage before they even get to the ravine that they either skip it or only shoot a single drive. This is a shame as the ravine does produce good birds, certainly not the equivalent of a top English shoot but as good as many normal UK shoots. These birds tend to be thirty to forty yards up and travelling with good speed.

Another reason why the birds do not fly particularly well is that birds tend to be blanked into the drives and often do not walk but fly in and this diminishes their capacity to fly well during the drive.

Lany

This was the 'Presidential shoot' under the Communists and continues today for hosting VIP governmental types. It is best and best known for its big game, especially stag, but does offer the best value of any of the Eastern European shoots. Again, these are not tall birds, but they are as good as most of the birds that I have seen in the East and better than some. It is also very close to Prague, which makes for a short run from a hotel in town. The gamekeeper actually speaks reasonably good English, while the manager speaks none, but good German. So if you go to this shoot, make sure that your agent speaks German so that plans can be made appropriately.

This is a very compact shoot where one walks from the lodge to each of the drives, and from drive to drive. This aspect is one of the reasons why the shoot has so much favour with politicians. The food was quite mediocre, ditto the wine and if I were shooting here again, I would definitely bring my own vino. The drives are not much below the lesser – aka usual – drives at Konopiste, for much less money; but not in the same class as Konopiste's best.

Castle Zidlochovice, near Brno, is perhaps Eastern Europe's most famous shoot, but bags tend to be in the 1,000 to 2,000 birds a day range and the minimum contract is for 800 birds a day whereas the shoots above have a minimum of 600 birds a day. I know some teams that have gone to Zidlochovice and have killed a couple of thousand birds a day and these 'sports' were not tall bird Shots. Zidlochovice has an area called the Russian valley where supposedly taller birds can be presented.

Hungary

I have shot Hungary a few times. The first time that I shot Hungary, about a decade ago, I went as the guest of a friend's company. The birds were low, so that except for one long crossing bird on the first drive – I was an end gun – I did not fire a shot, even though I could have killed fifty birds over me. The fellow who was running the shoot came over to me and asked me to kill birds as he needed to make the bag. I did so with great reluctance. The birds were the height of the trees. To be fair, it had been a year of great floods and everything was wet, including the birds, and a soaked pheasant does not fly at its best. But even in ideal conditions, these would have been medium birds. The other problem was that they tended to place the Guns much too close to the game crops being driven, primarily maize, and the birds did not have much time to rise before reaching the team. That said, it was good value for money.

Additionally, I had a near death experience. A mega rich IT guy had brought a friend of his from Holland. Unfortunately, this young Dutchman had never shot before and there were no proper minders, or as I recall a normal safety speech. On a drive on the first day with the birds coming out of a nearby game crop, I stood watching these non-shootable pheasants being presented. A pheasant flying at about five feet was coming between this Dutchman and me. To my astonishment he was raising the gun on the bird and had he fired, he would quite literally have taken my head off. When I saw him mounting the gun I shouted, 'Don't shoot' and simultaneously hit the deck. Luckily he heard me and did not fire. I walked over to him and told him if he pulled a stunt like that again, I would shoot in self defence. He was much more circumspect thereafter. (Another problem with these Eastern European shoots is that one is given a loader who encourages his Gun to shoot at everything, yelling, 'Shoot, shoot, shoot!'.) This encourages both the taking of poor quality birds and dangerous or unsportsmanlike shooting.

The duck shoot associated with this operator for flighted mallard was significantly better than the pheasant shooting. On some days we would stand on a dock in a big lake with birds coming over and on other days we would be in 'barrel' blinds, with the blinds screwed/anchored in the lake bottoms.

The accommodation was acceptable, but the food was too heavy and peasantine for my liking, goulash being their version of nouvelle cuisine and the lightest dish offered. (I like goulash, just not every day.)

The one great thing that came out of this shoot was that I met my amazing friend Tom Roulston, with whom I have enjoyed much sport around the world. (He and I got on in no little part because he was the only Gun on the trip who had shot much in Britain.)

The best pheasants in Hungary are presented in the hilly terrain north-east of Budapest.

Part V – North America

First Shot Outfitters aka A Dog Man's Quail Hunt
Vic Venters

Great dog work and lots of quail ought to go together like butter and biscuits but with wild bobwhite populations down by over eighty per cent over the last two decades throughout much of the bird's historic range, hunters have found their field fare pretty dry of late. Those seeking quail hunting like it used to be – wild birds aplenty shot over classic pointers – should look to Mike Wyatt's First Shot Outfitters, headquartered in Coleman County in north-west Texas. Sited just south of Rolling Plains country, Wyatt's operation offers a wide variety of hunting opportunities throughout the year – from spring turkey to dove to ducks to deer – but his first love is catering to discriminating quail hunters.

I first hunted with Wyatt back in the late '90s when he was guiding part-time for a large ranch near Guthrie, in Dickens County, Texas. During my first three-day bobwhite hunt Wyatt clearly proved the most successful guide on the ranch with the best dogs, and he consistently produced almost double the daily covey rises of other guides. My father, my uncle and myself were so impressed we've been repeat clients since, following Mike when he returned to full-time guiding and outfitting for himself. Now in his ninth year of operation, Wyatt is considered by many one of the best independent quail guides in Texas – which, given the state's size and bird-hunting traditions, sounds like big talk.

But I don't doubt it. Last year Texas suffered what was arguably its worst quail season in twenty years. A scorching summer and severe drought produced a disastrous breeding season through much of the state, especially for bobwhites. In a year in which many Texas wild-quail lodges simply cancelled their bookings, we were able to push fifteen to twenty coveys and take limits of fifteen birds daily – of blue quail mostly, with a handful of bobwhites tossed in. The latter have traditionally been Wyatt's staple but because he leases vast amounts of territory – more than 260,000 acres last year – he was able to move his hunters where the birds were, to West Texas where blue quail populations had held up much better than those of bobwhites.

This meant two-hour, crack-of-dawn rides from Wyatt's lodge into scalie country, and equally long return trips, but the truck time was worth it when you consider the alternatives. As has often been noted, the scaled quail is not a gentleman like Mister Bob – coveys run like rabbits and flush wilder and at longer range, with the singles often flying to the thickest prickly stuff this side of Br'er Rabbit's briar patch. Tighter-holding scalie singles offer closer shooting opportunities but hunters raised on bobwhites should expect a faster-paced hunt through harder terrain than they might typically be used to, though not all of the rangeland will be as cactus-studded as some of that we hunted through.

This year the long rides will be a thing of the past as Wyatt has just opened a satellite lodge near Sweetwater and Colorado City, which is much closer to his West Texas leases. He has also added more land, and now controls a staggering 350,000-plus acres around the Sweetwater operation. In bobwhite country around Coleman, Wyatt leases 60,000 acres, which is hunted from his purpose-built 2,000-square-foot lodge of Douglas fir logs built in 2005. With two bedrooms, a loft and two bathrooms, and a great room with a cavernous rock fireplace, the lodge has an intimate, rustic feel about it. I have not seen the new Sweetwater lodge but according to Wyatt it is a refurbished farmhouse, 'very clean and comfortable'.

Each of the lodges sleeps nine – or three parties of three. A group of nine is required to book each lodge fully for themselves; otherwise separate parties will share the lodge. Including himself, Wyatt has six guides working for him; each has at least twelve fully trained dogs and is equipped with a rigged-out ATV for transporting hunters, dogs and guides. Typically parties comprise two to three (max) hunters per ATV. Wyatt and his guides typically run two pointers on the ground simultaneously, sometimes just one dog if the blues are especially jumpy. Expect top-flight dog work – Wyatt is uncompromising in his selection and training of dogs. Each guide also has a retriever to assist in finding downed birds though Wyatt reports Lexie, his black Lab, 'points as many singles as my pointers'. (Yes, Lexie does point!) Wyatt is careful with his wild-bird resource, allowing three bobwhites to be taken from a covey before moving on to find another; a couple more birds can be taken from blue-quail coveys, which tend to be larger. Bobwhites in Coleman are typically hunted in and around pastures; blue and bobs to the west in everything from open rangeland to pastures.

In a normal year hunters typically average pushing twenty-plus bobwhite coveys per day; two years ago in a spectacular season it averaged well over thirty. Last year around Coleman bobwhite populations were so depressed Wyatt rarely hunted them. In a good year blues in West Texas can be so abundant that if hunters can shoot well personal limits should be had by lunch.

The good news is that this summer's abundant rains have produced dramatically better habitat conditions for both bobwhites around Coleman and blues and bobs out west. Populations are expected to rebound substantially; how much so will not be known until hunters hit the fields. Nonetheless Wyatt is confident of a good year, especially near Sweetwater where bobwhites should make up a greater percentage of the bag than last year's scalie-dominated crop.

Expect to eat well in Wyatt's care. In the standard package all meals are provided and hunters normally return to the lodge for lunch and dinner. Mike's wife, Monica, is the cook at the Coleman lodge, and a good enough one to be featured in Tosh Brown's new cookbook *Grazing Across Texas*, which featured recipes from ranches and sporting lodges across the state. Lunch might be fried quail with gravy and all the fixings; dinner might be mesquite-grilled rib-eye steaks or chicken-fried steak, finished with a bevy of homemade cookies, pies or almond-layered bread pudding. Wyatt provides beer but guests should bring their own wine or liquor to the lodge. For those who can't quite leave business back in the big city, Wyatt's lodge has internet access, landline telephone and fax, and a copy machine. Satellite TV provides a fix for the sports-addicted.

Most of First Shot's business is word-of-mouth and repeat customers and December dates, in particular, tend to be booked long in advance.

The nearest commercial airport is Abilene, a forty-five-minute drive from Coleman and about an hour and a half from Sweetwater. Parties may rent their own transportation or arrange with the Wyatts for a shuttle service, a cost-effective option that can accommodate four to six hunters.

Cartridges are not provided as part of the package but is readily available in Abilene for the wingshooters who arrive by air – though those with exotic shotshell needs (such as short 2½ inch cartridges) should ship ahead of time to the lodge. Small bores are suitable for the bobwhites under normal conditions though late-season blues are best tackled with 12-gauges – and be sure to bring some tighter chokes if your gun has screw-ins. I like No. 7.5 shot for all round Texas quail shooting, though some argue No. 6 shot appropriate for blues flushing at longer ranges.

Non-residents are required to purchase a $45 small-game licence. For more information or to purchase online: http://www.tpwd.state.tx.us/business/licenses/online_sales/

Wild birds are always unpredictable, as are their populations, but I have never been surprised by Mike's work ethic. Simply put, he and his guides will hustle to give his clients a great bird hunt over fine dogs from sunup to sundown.

Big Spring Texas
Clinton Smullyan

W ild quail has been the American sport of kings for most of the twentieth century. Oilmen, grand inheritors, masterful industrialists, and bankers, old money and new alike acquired large swathes of the best quail country in the United States and enjoyed it in a leisurely fashion, in fine clothes, on polished wagons, with kennels full of finely tuned well-bred English pointers, with packs of attendants in tow, and it can still be enjoyed in that manner. But the wild quail tradition includes millions of farmers and townsmen, cowboys and ranchers, plainsmen and plain folks who have sufficient inclination to train a dog, buy or borrow a shotgun, and hunt. And that is also the truly traditional way to chase quail – it is a classless sport that can be dressed for a palace or a shack without affecting its centre.

I have shot quail on great plantations where the owner's house is old, huge and filled with fine things, where there are large staffs of workers to manage magnificent horses, pristine mule-drawn wagons and elaborate meals, where 'Yes sir, No sir, Oh sir and Please sir' prevail (apologies to Rudyard Kipling). I shot for years on a magnificent private property in Florida owned by American royalty that was sold recently for half a billion dollars. I have shot quail on famous South Texas ranches owned by grand Texas names like King and Kennedy, and in Florida where the Guns arrived by helicopter directly to the field. But there is something preternaturally American about wild quail hunting (not 'shooting' as in England) and once one is on the ground, there is no social status to note. Much of Oklahoma and West Texas especially engage the hunter in an environment that is close to the earth and distanced from pretence.

It is to West Texas, near Midland, that we have travelled, four native New Yorkers and one from the tailored province of Greenwich, Connecticut. The drive from Midland airport is all visibly Southwest – drilling rigs, water pumps, barbecue joints and generator lots by the highway and sweeping horizons beyond are our view. But well within an hour we are far from any hint of population density, surrounded by scrubland decorated with huge bales of cotton and white-sprinkled, picked-over cotton-fields, giving a spare pointillist background.

We arrive at Buffalo Springs Ranch owned by John Cox of Game Management Services. Highly professional and thoroughly amusing, Cox and his partner Jerry Woods are good at everything, from mesquite grilled steaks (local beef, local mesquite) to gracefully helping an over-large over-aged graceless oaf (the author) onto a comfortable western trooper saddle. Both Cox and Woods are deeply knowledgeable graduate wildlife biologists who consult widely and are fine teachers if one chooses to ask about this simultaneously rich and spare environment. They are also skilled good-old-boys in tune with that ancient Texas tradition, another pleasure to be consumed.

Although we are a group of five city-bred fellows, we have been shooting together for from fifteen to nearly fifty years, and are pleased to be getting to live Cox's dream as well as our own. Cox has just built a splendidly Western, woody 'great house' and a ten-bedroom adjunct. All the rooms are panelled with handsome pine and all the furniture has been made to Cox's exacting specifications from a lovely timber, all defined by a Southwest aesthetic vocabulary, good quality and comfort.

It is at this lodge where the twenty-first century intervenes in an ancient sport, and I am very pleased that it does. Each room has its en-suite bathroom and shower with endless hot water, not only an improvement on the nineteenth century, but on many grand English 'Stately Home' shoots. The nineteenth century frontier rhythm is full of romantic charm when in the saddle on the prairie, but indoor plumbing and good air-conditioning are a fine comfort at the end (beginning and middle) of the day. So is good food. Buffalo Springs Ranch can give you the authentic nineteenth century rhythm in the field, but, as a fine comedienne wrote, 'I am not one of those people who want to return to the land. I am one of those people who wants to return to the hotel.'

The next morning, fed and provisioned, mounted on well-trained horses, we are out on that great American prairie.

It's only an hour's drive from Midland airport but a planetary system away from New York. The land is scrubby with spiky mesquite and native grasses, some cactus, sand and red clay, every inch rich with the desert vocabulary scratching and scrambling for life. There are no pen-raised or released birds here; the land is without excess and every creature, every flora, lives to the limits of its own envelope of survival.

One of the joys of Buffalo Springs Ranch is that once we have saddled up and ridden out there is little evidence of recent centuries; we have engaged the rhythm of the American frontier, arriving at the shooting part of the property on horseback, with shotguns in saddle scabbards, following our dogs, pursuing our quarry just as the nineteenth century inhabitants did when they sought quail for the table.

The buffalo were here first and dramatically. The great beasts, which dominated the area two centuries ago, left their mark on this land with some remarkable evolutionary herd engineering. At mid-morning, we are standing on the edge of a buffalo wallow trampled into a hard-packed, dish-shaped basin by the snorting, weighty, legendary herds to collect the sparse rainfall for herd survival. 100 years ago? 200? Time is irrelevant and inevident.

Dismounted, guns in hand, we know the birds are nearby because Jack, the world's best English setter, tells us so and we have learned that distrusting Jack's nose is a sure way to look foolish.

And we are in perfect suspense: Jack and an English pointer are both locked on point – rigid and quivering simultaneously. The warming Texas morning has only the subtle sounds of creaking saddle leather and susurrus of wind through mesquite. The immediate universe is taut and tensioned. Time hangs, charged, intense, condensed. Then, a climactic rush, a splendid moment of blasted motion, a staccato-metered roar, faster than the conscious – a cloud of quail are explosively in flight, and have rocketed away in a gorgeous, pulsative, noise-filled instant. My son Alex and I fire four shots, three birds fall and the adrenaline content of all of Glasscock County, Texas, has been significantly elevated. The birds are gone in a fraction of a startled breath. It doesn't matter how often I have experienced it, standing gasping in the middle of a covey rise of wild quail is a moment suffused with sudden glory.

We pick up our quarry, three blue quail, remount and move on, settling in the saddles as our heartbeats normalize.

I have friends in Texas who are otherwise fine sportsmen, but claim that blue quail are the only birds they shoot because they hate the bird. In a normal year in this scrub country, blues will demonstrate their preference for running rather than flying and the hunter, legs bloody, punctured and torn in the pursuit, will have to chase the blues long distances on foot, cursing the cactus spikes and hypodermic needles of the mesquite bushes, before the birds will fly. This year, however, there was an exotically large amount of rain in the summer and the native grasses have grown too thick for the blues to run easily, so we have found coveys holding steadily in place where the dogs first find them. I do prefer Gentleman Bob, the bobwhite quail, which usually have the courtesy to hold awhile when the dogs are pointing, so one does not have to chase them. In this part of Texas hunters can expect to find both blues and bobs in identical cover.

The quail are ingrained with their predator defences – for the blues it is to run from the hunters until out of shotgun range and then fly safely out of sight. For my preferred bobwhite, the defence is to burst out of cover in large groups with a startling noise and then criss-cross in flight to confuse the eye of raptor or man.

On our second day of shooting, three of us, experienced quail shots all, are standing perfectly spaced behind a lovely pointer frozen on point, as a covey of more than thirty bobwhite quail rise in front of us, in two distinct flights a few seconds apart, and within twenty feet of where we are planted. Six shots are fired, six easy-can't-miss-shots into a cloud of birds; no birds are hit, perhaps none even frightened. Several very naughty compound biological unlikelihoods are loudly proclaimed. Each of us has made the quails' defence effective by allowing our eyes to be distracted by a bird going one way, whilst having started by moving our barrels towards a bird going another. That means, collectively, three-quarters of a pound of lead has been expended to try to bring down a bird that weighs considerably less. Shame engulfs us, as does admiration; if you love the sport, you cheer for the birds.

At the end of each day we are engulfed in comfort in the great house, in the bedrooms and in the basic, excellent comestibles.

What gives Buffalo Springs Ranch the potential of a truly great shoot? It possesses a rare combination of completely wild birds, good horses, fine dog work, extremely comfortable facilities, knowledgeable hosts and a reasonably accessible location.

However, the heart of a great shoot is to combine those qualities of sport and venue with the rich rewards of friendship. John Cox and Buffalo Springs Ranch consistently do the former; my sons and my splendid friends take care of the latter joyously. Bravo all.

The Ledges Inn on the Miramichi
Vic Venters

The sun was out and the sky blue on a crisp afternoon in October as we pulled into the drive at the Ledges Inn, overlooking New Brunswick's much-storied Miramichi River. I had no sooner walked to the river's edge to stretch my legs when a salmon the size of my thigh broached in the pool below me, landing with a heavy *ker-splash*. We were there to hunt birds, not to fish, but my wife, Leigh, and my father couldn't help but notice the Cheshire grin I brought back to the car.

The next morning my father and I sat in pouring rain beside a bogan, a shallow oxbow pond elsewhere known as a slough. We weren't wet long, though, as twenty minutes later we had our combined limit of six black ducks, each retrieved with aplomb by Niner, our guide's feckless Irish setter.

The sun poked through the clouds a few hours later as we were floating a wilderness tributary of the Miramichi, canoe-hopping with guide Bill Hooper and Niner from one abandoned homestead to another. We hunted fields grown up with poplar, alder and thorn apple, and in them found the concentrations of woodcock for which this maritime province is famous. The next day brought more of the same: vigorous sunshine, more ducks and a woodcock covert full of birds and large enough to hunt all day. For Manfred, my shorthair, it was a field of dreams, with more than enough woodcock to make up for his more than occasional outbreaks of excessive enthusiasm.

The Ledges Inn, in Doaktown, is a 6,000-square foot lodge owned and operated by Everett and Caroline St Pierre Taylor. It's built of handsome Eastern cedar and, with seven rooms and accommodations for fourteen, is a legitimate four-star lodge. Although The Ledges dates only from 1996, Everett's family has been in the Miramichi guiding and lodging business for seven generations. Caroline is Quebecois, from Montreal, and her French heritage was deliciously evident each night in her eclectic cuisine – Thai food one night, traditional roasts with perfectly cooked local vegetables another.

The Ledges was founded primarily as an upscale lodge for salmon anglers, but the Taylors also cater for discerning wingshooters in the fall. Unlike some of the older and bigger operations on the Miramichi, The Ledges has but four salmon pools out front – good water, mind you, but limited. The Taylors have compensated by specializing in float trips down most of the thirty-seven major tributaries that flow into the Miramichi, most of which have very limited access – and little or no hunting or fishing pressure.

They're able to do this largely thanks to partner Bill Hooper, formerly the chief fisheries biologist for the province. Not only does Hooper know the lay of virtually all the salmon pools in these rivers, but forty years of floating them has allowed him to 'research' many of the grouse and woodcock coverts along their banks.

During our three days we never saw another hunter – anyone, for that matter – on the rivers we floated. What we did encounter were woodcock aplenty in streamside coverts, with enough grouse flushing here and there to test the dogs. I know of nothing more cathartic than drifting a pristine river plaited in autumn's finest foliage with an able guide poling the canoe. By trip's end I had left my stresses and worries swirling downriver and had a game bag plump with unforgettable memories.

New York Duck and Geese on Long Island

The Long Island waterfowl hunter has three options: hire a guide, outfit himself on the bays, or hunt in controlled public gunning areas. These opportunities can provide good shooting for broadbills, blacks, mallards and sea ducks as well as geese.

Short Course for Long Island Waterfowling

'Is 4 am late at night or early in the morning?' I thought as I walked from my apartment building to my car, which was parked at the far end of the street on which I live. There are few things that will induce me to rise at 3 am and drive for two hours. Waterfowl hunting is one of them.

Although I live in New York City, I am fortunate to live near the good duck hunting along much of Long Island, and goose shooting as good, in some pockets, as any found on the East Coast. Many species, particularly Canada Geese, are increasing in numbers here, although the shooting is not what it was at the turn of the century.

In the glory days of American waterfowling, days when market gunners would shoot carloads of ducks, there was no better area along the Eastern seaboard for hunting than Long Island. Rich Park Avenue types formed clubs and bought or leased prime lands so they could hunt the area in gentlemanly fashion. And the serious hunters designed and refined gunning boats. Masterful decoy carvers, perhaps unaware of the posthumous treasures that they were creating, plied their craft.

But the great flocks of birds that blackened the sky and blanketed the water are no more. The market gunners are long gone, and few prestigious clubs remain. (A number of clubs and preserves were claimed as eminent domain about forty years ago; some are now public fishing or hunting areas.) Still the traditions continue with recent master decoy carvers, such as Bob Hand, and classic guides like George Combs.

George Combs offered a unique service that takes one back in time to the days of the market hunters. Unlike most guides who shoot from floating blinds, shore blinds or pits, George hunted from a gunning boat (also called a layout or punting boat) such as ones the old-time hunters used. George's great-grandfathers were market hunters, men who stalked large rafts of birds, killing with punting guns (a large fowling piece, up to four-gauge, which could kill many birds with one shot) and shipping their wares to the best restaurants of New York.

This day when I shot with him, we towed the gunning boats by skiff to the western end of the Great South Bay, within view of the Jones Beach Tower. The main advantage of this method is mobility. It's possible to predict where the birds will be, based on the tides and the weather, and set up there.

Leaving the skiff anchored in deep water, we travelled by gunning boats to a small strip of land where we set the boats in among the sea grass. George quickly set out the decoys: Canada geese at the left, black ducks in the middle, broadbills on the right.

We lay down in the boats, which were camouflaged by salt-grass thatching, and waited. Bufflehead skimmed across the water, out of range. Brant (no relation) frequently flew in range, but these were protected birds so we didn't shoot. Then a black duck came out of the east and was about to land in our stool when we sat up to shoot. It quickly veered off, and I did not connect until my third shot. Shooting from a sitting position is not difficult, but not having done it before, I rushed my first two shots.

The unseasonably warm weather that the Northeast was experiencing that fall through the first half of December had made hunting less fruitful than normal. We did bag two more black ducks, the only birds that came to our decoys, and missed a passing shot at canvasback.

You'll probably need a blind or a boat to successfully hunt the rest of the island. The bay side of Barrier Beach along the south shore of Long Island offers good shooting, particularly for black ducks. 'But the trick to success,' according to Steven Sanford, a wildlife biologist with the New York Department of Environmental Conservation, 'is a four-wheel-drive with lots of pull to get your boat and trailer in and out'. A good seaworthy duck boat is essential. The one problem in the area is that parking is limited, so you will have to scout the area ahead of the season.

Long Island sea duck shooting is largely an untapped resource, says Sanford. 'A boat with a tarp is sufficient for success, and access is easy from any north-shore harbour into the sound.' The Peconic Bay and The Sound offer good sea duck hunting well before any other waterfowling opens. White-winged scoters and old-squaw predominate at that time. During the regular season mergansers and golden-eyes broaden the bag. Bob Hand, one of the most dedicated and experienced gunners on the island, agrees wholeheartedly. 'You've got to know the water and your equipment. The sea can look calm when you go out. Then if the wind and tide change, you get a riptide and the boat lands in your face.'

The sea duck season runs from late September through mid-January in the waters of Long Island Sound, Peconic Bay east of a line from Miamogue Point to Red Cedar Point, and the Atlantic Ocean. Experienced hunters use 12-gauge shotguns with three-inch magnum shells. Some have gone to 3½ inch, which makes sense now that non-toxic shot is required. Hevi-shot or, indeed, any tung-sten-based load is most lethal. It may not be suitable for all shotguns however.

Southampton Township, which includes Shinnecock Bay, Hampton Bays Mecox Bay and others, requires town residency to anchor a boat or a blind. Much of the best shooting takes place in this area. If you're not a resident, you'll have to hire a guide or make friends with a native.

For mobility, a boat is unbeatable. The ideal craft is a classic gunning or layout boat, thatched with natural grass. With it you can hunt from Lawrence to Jones Beach to Captree Island in Great South Bay for black ducks one week, in the flats of Fire Island the following week, and chase broadbills in the deeper sections of the bay (Islip/Bayshore) later in the year. The deeper areas are less prone to icing up, and the birds tend to congregate in those regions.

The goose shooting on Long Island is excellent in limited areas. The prime areas are the potato fields of Southampton and Bridgehampton. This is privately controlled.

See the guides in Appendix 2.

Mexico's Laguna Madre
Don Terrell

oly smoke, we're under attack!' It was an announcement I made wide-eyed, as I watched the scene play before me. My shooting partner, Jim, just grinned, and replied, 'We'll handle it!' Thirty redhead ducks had come from nowhere, swooping from their high vantage point down through our decoys like kamikazes. They came in so fast and unexpectedly that neither of us managed to do more than feign a response. Our guide, Juan, chuckled, and added in his self taught English, 'You betta be ready! *They fast!*'

The second group was different. We could actually hear them before we saw them. Though still in the recovery phase when the dots appeared, similar in size to the last one, led by a fully plumed drake – bold red head shining in the afternoon sun – we were ready. Since the birds were attacking from the right and I was on the left, protocol required me to shoot the lead bird, as they crossed the decoys, with my partner starting about midway in the flock. I raised my Beretta 390, got the lead bird in my sights, and slapped the trigger. To my amazement, the two birds following the lead bird fell into the decoys. I actually didn't hear my partner shoot, but another bird fell in the back of the pack. I was so discombobulated that I did not shoot the second time. The guide was doubled over, laughing at us. 'They fast!' I looked at Jim. 'How many times did you shoot?' 'Just once, 'cause nothing I shot at fell. Some poor bird in the back of the flock got cooked, but nothing I shot at! I think I agree with Juan. *They fast!*'

We were not novices at duck shooting. We had hunted mallards and wood ducks back home for years, occasionally shot a few ringnecks, but big divers were a new experience. These birds were different. They didn't float into the decoys like a mallard. They just busted straight in and plopped down in the decoys. No circling, checking for errors in your layout, or any other defence. They saw the decoys, assumed they were part of the massive migration in the area, and just zoomed right in. It did take us a while to adjust to their bravado and speed, but soon we were leading them sufficiently and actually taking the birds we were targeting.

This was our first afternoon of shooting ducks in a truly magical place, Mexico's Laguna Madre. This expansive brackish water nutrient-filled estuary stretches south from above Corpus Christi, deep along Mexico's east coast for hundreds of miles. It is famous for its shrimp and redfish, but for me, the most important occupants of the Laguna Madre were the tens of thousands of migrating ducks that had been camping out along this watery corridor.

This is the primary wintering ground of the redhead duck, and on my first visit, I marvelled at the unbelievable flocks of ducks rafting along the shoreline and in the middle of the Laguna. We saw rafts of ducks estimated at more than five thousand birds as we cruised in the shrimpers' boats up and down the waterway. They wouldn't even move, unless you headed the boat into them, content to watch the boats go harmlessly by. The birds and the shrimpers enjoyed a very peaceful co-existence until some duck hunting explorer realized they were out there. Some hunting had been enjoyed, by a fortunate few, for years, but in the eighties, commercial hunting operations sprang up along the Laguna, taking advantage of the abundance of ducks resting there, far away from the duck hunter's usual venue, the inland ponds.

The Laguna is massive in some spots, dotted with islands, some large enough to support fresh water ponds, which fill with rainwater, particularly during the hurricane season. It's a complicated territory and an environment in which one can very easily become disoriented and lost. The savviest outfitters appealed to the commercial fishermen and shrimpers to find the ducks and also to take the hunters to them. They knew the Laguna like the backs of their hands, and knew where they were even in the dark. They also knew where all the shrimp nets and traps were, and could navigate the area without harming either. Since duck hunting is one of the sports where you need to be where you're going to hunt before daylight, the outfitters could depend on the native fishermen and shrimpers to navigate the boats from the lodges to the shooting areas without difficulty. Some of them even became guides, but for the most part, the pair of shooters would be accompanied by a boat driver and an experienced professional guide.

The boatmen were an interesting lot. I experienced the fishermen and shrimpers in a small village called Carbonera, right on the west bank of the Laguna Madre, due east of San Fernando, in the State of Tamaulipas. The village was accessible via the only paved road to the coast for miles north or south. Since it was the only paved road in the area, it was also patrolled incessantly by the military and local police in their attempts to control drug traffic from offshore. This caused frequent anxiety among my American comrades, who were inexperienced in staring at a machine-gun manned by someone who looked at least twelve. A simple misunderstanding could have been eventful. We eventually got accustomed to seeing the police, but never got comfortable with the machine-gun-wielding teenagers. They constantly checked our permits and vehicle contents, but most aggravating situations could be managed with a few photos of Presidents Hamilton and Jackson placed in the proper hands.

My favourite among the commercial lodges we visited was just beyond the village of Carbonera, and was in stark contrast to the fishing village. We had electricity, vats of potable water, well built cottages, soft beds, a full bar, and lots of staff. It was one of the greatest places to experience duck hunting on the North American continent. We Yanks would fly into McAllen or Harlingen, Texas, arriving in time to spend the first night at a pleasant and comfortable hotel in one of those towns. We could explore the native cuisine in either of these border area towns, enjoying animated conversation about the venture ahead of us. Like youngsters, hardly any of us slept, due to the anticipation of the coming day. After breakfast, we were picked up by a fine luxury touring bus and driven across the border into Mexico. Advance preparation and professional administrative services provided by the outfitter made this trip seamless. The journey on the bus was full of animated conversation between the visitors, who were not necessarily all from the same group. The outfitter had separate operations in the area, and the bus served both areas. In addition to the duck hunting we normally preferred, there was also plenty hunting for wild quail, dove shooting, and goose hunting, primarily on the interior east of our chosen coastal setting. Less than two hours of riding, making new friends, chatting with your buddies from home, watching videos of the many shooting adventures offered by your host, and an occasional nap, brought you to the first camp, just outside San Fernando. We would all get off the bus, stretch, and grab an absolutely delicious margarita and either a nacho or quesadilla, both unmatched by anything produced in the USA. The mariachi band playing in the background added another splendid touch to the welcome. After a few minutes of relaxation and frivolity, we boarded another vehicle, which took us to our waterfront destination.

After lunch, we quickly got into our hunting gear, which consisted of anything with a dark camo look, the thinnest long-sleeve camo shirt you could find, and your hipboots. The walk to the boats was about fifty yards. It was hot as blazes, but you always took a jacket with you because the boat ride back would be after dark and sometimes quite chilly.

The Laguna is a challenge for the deep V-hulled boats, since in some areas it is extremely shallow. The boatmen and guides had to push the boat into deeper water to run the motor, and I enjoyed helping them, over their protests. It was considered their job, and we were the guests. Nice touch. The guide and boatman had already worked out where we would be going that afternoon. The guide would recognize it when we arrived, but had no idea how to get there, or more specifically, how to get back after dark.

Once we arrived at our destination, the guide and boatman really went to work. They always built a brand-new blind every time we went out. Sometimes they would steal cover from a blind they passed on the way, but most often, they would disappear into the distance, returning with huge piles of cut brush on their shoulders. They mostly carried a bench with them in the boat. If they were going to an area where the mud was so soft it was impossible to stand up without getting shorter by the minute, they would carry a bench and a standing platform. They would build this elaborate fresh growth blind around the two hunters, providing the best shooting cover I have ever seen. They would thrust the stem of the branches in the mud, providing a well-brushed cover, back and front for the shooters. The hunters would enter the blind and the impromptu contractors would modify it to your particular height. When you sat down, you were totally invisible. When you stood up, you had a perfect shooting area in front of you. Building a blind for me was a particular challenge for them, since I am short, but they always made it right, with lots of banter aimed at my proximity to the ground. You always had to be sure of your footing, since you were in mud, and turning on a bird provided some wonderful opportunities for showmanship, both with the occasional spectacular shot, but most often with you pirouetting into the brush while your feet rigidly stayed put, interfering with your spectacular shot. After we had become somewhat settled in our blind, the guide would hide just inside our blind, or just outside the blind. The boatman would ride off into the sun, looking for birds and getting out of our way.

The guides were excellent callers of the pintails, but calling redheads is more difficult. It's like calling cats. Works better if you're where you've seen them sitting or feeding earlier. If you found a spot where the redheads were working, they would dive into your setup with reckless abandon. Since the drakes are boldly coloured, it is rarely difficult to pick them out. The sunny skies in Mexico are a great help, and the colours on the heads of the redhead drakes just shimmy in the sun. Such a beautiful sight. We might shoot a few redheads, then wait a while for the pintails, which the guide had promised would come in a bit later. He did not lie!

The first three just sailed in from afar, and we let some redheads actually land in the decoys while waiting for more pintails. They stayed for a while, got uncomfortable, and set off for another resting spot. The pintails started drifting in. Singles and pairs at first, then larger groups appeared before us. We chose to shoot only drakes, since the bird appeared to be having some difficulty in the breeding grounds. The drakes are truly one of our noblest of birds. Its profile is slim and elegant. Its colours, although mostly brown and white, are put together in such a splendid arrangement, complemented by the iridescent green wing spectrum, and the beautiful bold white stripe intruding on the coffee-coloured head. In the air, the pintail is the quintessential ballet dancer, flawless in its move-ments, weightlessly balancing itself on the currents, gliding effortlessly into the decoys.

This bird is a thing of unmistakable beauty, and one of my favourite vistas in the outdoors. It's a great contrast to the redheads, who, coming to the decoys, resemble a bunch of burley dockworkers attacking on Harley's.

Guides were also accomplished retrievers, since there were no dogs to retrieve downed birds. How they could walk that far in the boot-gobbling mud always amazed me. I've even watched them chase wounded ducks, lightly dancing through the mud. They made it look so easy that I ventured out to help. With the second step, I was absolutely trapped in mud midway up my calf. I remained precariously there until the guide came over, grinning, and lifted me out of the muck and aided me back to the blind. His advice, 'You stay in the blind', was well heeded for the rest of our time on the Laguna.

We shot pretty well, but on one occasion, etched in my mind, a drake redhead, with a broken wing, managed to get away from us and swam, out of range, toward an island a couple of football fields away. I was watching the bird get farther and farther from us, when something in my far vision attracted my attention. I looked closely, beyond the escaping duck, to the island where he was headed, and I was in for a surprise. The surprise to me was waiting to surprise the duck on arrival. A coyote was crouched on the shoreline, just beyond the water's edge, almost lying down flat. The bird, oblivious to his presence, continued to swim toward his worst nightmare. As the bird entered the even more shallow water of the surf, the coyote darted out into the water, grabbed the bird, and trotted off along the water's edge and disappeared behind the vegetation. We saw lots of coyotes during our visit to the Laguna, but this was the only time, over many years, that I actually saw one take a live duck. We did see lots of duck bones left from coyote meals and we would occasionally have a hawk land on a downed bird and completely eat the bird before we had time to pick it up. I will not comment on our shooting prowess that sunny afternoon, but will only say we did have a pintail drake or two to show the fellows and a nice string of redheads. We had also picked up two widgeon out of a flock of six, and that's all I'm going to reveal about that!

The birds were a treat and while the redheads and pintails were the most abundant species, we also had great fun with the green winged teal, widgeon, gadwalls, lesser scaup, shovellers, and the occasional canvasback, blue winged teal, cinnamon teal and mottled duck, or Mexican duck. The latter looks just like our black duck, but the colour of the head is lighter and the colour spectrum on the wings is more green than purple. The shooting on the Laguna has never been a disappointment and I have loved every trip I've enjoyed there over many years, and not all the excitement of this area hunt takes place on the Laguna itself. The surrounding area is farmland, and miles of grain fields cover this area, hosting many other winged species. The duck shooting on inland ponds along the Laguna is wonderful. Wild quail hunting while dodging cactus and rattlesnakes is also among the best shooting available anywhere.

I have seen thousands of geese, including snows, blues, lesser Canada, Ross' and specklebellies hover and drop into our spread. It's truly one of the grandest wingshooting experiences anywhere in the world.

On this particularly boring late morning, I was alone in my observations. Even the guides and bird boys were napping. In the distance, I saw a lone goose flying in our direction, but he was a very long ways from us, and I doubted he would continue coming to us. I continued to watch him, and he had seen the decoys and he was coming. I came up with what I thought was a true inspiration at the time. This is a great opportunity for a photo, so what I need to do is wake up my friend, get him ready, and I'll get down in the blind and take a photo of him shooting the goose. Sounded totally clever to me. I punched my friend and told him, 'There's a lone goose coming. Get up and shoot him and I'm going to take your picture.' He staggered somnambulantly to his feet and I pointed out the winged warrior to him. He was ready for action. Remember, no one else is awake. The bird slowly and methodically continues to head our way, until it is super obvious his flight is going to be interrupted by a loud noise. The bird gets just about over the blind, when I realize I will not be able to get the photo, because there is too much blind material in my way. Loud noise. My friend makes a good shot on the bird, and it falls far enough away to give the bird boy exercise after his rudely interrupted nap. Of course, all the sleeping beauties have had their nocturnal pleasures interrupted and have popped out of their blinds, wild eyed. 'What happened?' is the primary cry, and we go to explaining that I had raised my friend from a dead sleep for the photo opt and the super shot I had hoped to capture, and Ed had nicely shot the goose, without the benefit of my photo record of the feat. By the time everyone had regained their composure, the bird boy returned with the now deceased bird, and I got immediately sick. There was a big blue plastic band around the specklebelly's neck, and bands on both legs. If I had only kept quiet and taken the bird myself, I would be the proud new owner of all those bands, the wingshooter's grand prize and dream. The grand trophy of success in waterfowling – the bird band! I had let this golden opportunity pass me by, all for want of a photo, which I did not get.

The first time I hunted geese in the Laguna Madre area was a unique experience for me. We were hunting in a grain sorghum field, but not near water, just out in the field. It was a field where geese had been feeding the day before and our guide was confident they would return. We were settled in the pits before daylight, and I was waiting for the early flight. Nothing happened. I was quite disappointed, since I had really been looking forward to this experience, after hearing tales from my friends. I finally lifted my head and asked one of my companions, 'Do you think we've been skunked?' I think I woke up the guide, who muttered, 'Geese fly late.' Well, I pondered, if geese fly late, why did we not sleep late? It was broad daylight and almost 8 am when I noticed an interesting cloud miles away from us. It almost appeared to be wavering. Not blessed with the best of eyesight, I just took my eyes off it for a while and focused on other boring terrain around me. When I wandered back to the cloud, it was much bigger, and the guide said, incredibly slowly, 'Get down. Geese coming.'

The cloud kept coming and getting bigger for what seemed like hours, until finally I could see that it was geese. This was a huge flock of geese and they seemed about 30,000 feet up and set to pass over us without ever acknowledging we were there. They kept coming, until they were directly over us, and my heart stopped beating. The geese were slowing down. They were still in the stratosphere, but they slowed almost to a dead stop. No one said a word. Hidden in my well covered blind, with my well masked face, I peeped up through the stalks to see what was happening. What I saw, I will never forget. These birds from Heaven had stopped far above us and were sitting like kites. All of a sudden, they started dropping out of the sky, tumbling and turning in complete cartwheels in unimaginable aerobatic manoeuvres that are etched permanently in my brain; freefalling until they were just above our decoys. They floated, lightly using their wings, across the decoys looking for the proper place to sit, back and forth. There were hundreds of them, all trying to find a place to alight. I had forgotten the wait, and my anxiety was no longer just to shoot, but to watch this unique moment in the outdoors.

I was incredibly excited at what I was seeing, and the interruption of 'Shoot 'em' stunned me into action. I popped up through the stalks and had a choice of fifty different birds to shoot, and my mind was stumbling through the complicated analysis until I finally selected the first bird. My first ever snow goose hit the dirt. I shot another snow and a spec, reloaded and shot a spec going away before collapsing, exhausted into the pit. My heart was racing, and my thoughts were not on the birds I had just put on the ground, but on the once in a lifetime treat enjoyed by my eyes.

That was not the only flock of birds to visit us that morning, but I really don't remember the others.

The Laguna Madre is still one of the premier waterfowl destinations in the world, but the increased use of airboats has the birds much more unsettled than during my early visits. While we were accustomed to passing very close to mammoth rafts of ducks, it is now very unusual to get within a half mile of them without putting them to flight. The redheads are still there, but many have decided to rest off shore during the day, returning to the Laguna to feed.

I have enjoyed hunting all over the world, but most of my favourite duck hunting memories are here on the Laguna Madre.

Part VI – South America

Duck in Argentina: Buenos Aires Bound

Figuratively, 5:00 am came earlier than usual. The day before we had been shooting dove in the province of Cordoba. Working on a tight schedule, we shot the eared dove early in the day, returned to the lodge for lunch, chartered a plane from Cordoba airport to Buenos Aires, and drove another hour south to Los Patos, the appropriately named ranch in San Miguel del Monte. Dinner began at 10. Then, once again, into the arms of Morpheus.

Breakfast passed quickly and quietly. By 6:00 am we were outside, dressed in waders and waterfowl gear. The guides fetched our shotguns from the gun room. It was nearly a forty-minute drive though probably only five to ten miles as the crow flies. We left the main road and turned down a dirt or mud road pitted by too many drivers cutting cross-country when it was wet. Torn up badly, it limited our speed. Nutria crossed the track. Some say their meat is delicious. I, who have been known to eat lion, draw the line on rodents. I do admit that their fur is lovely. Someone said that the species is not a rodent. They look like a giant round-faced rat to me.

The moon was full, and very bright. A few clouds formed eerie shapes. To paraphrase Bela Lugosi: 'The children of the night were, no doubt, happy.'

We arrived at the small pond. In the darkness we made last-minute adjustments and walked a hundred yards or so, the last forty through the puddle, to a clump of grass, junco reed, like bulrush about twenty yards wide. We sat on metal stools stuck in the mud. I place my shells on a large clump of dry grass, a mini island, if you will, to my left.

As my two companions Chuck Larsen and Kirk Kelly and I settled in, our guides – Brian and Paco – set out the decoys.

Brian's dad is one of Chuck Larsen's best friends. Indeed, they have hunted every year for the last forty-three seasons except for one when Chuck was in the army. Brian has guided for three years in Argentina from March through September. During the 'other' hunting season, he returns to Burnt Pines, which Chuck owns, one of the best and most successful whitetail deer and quail plantations in the South, situated close to Atlanta.

Brian is very helpful and well spoken, a recent graduate of the University of Wisconsin. While guiding is relatively new to him, he grew up hunting North Dakota and the prairie provinces of Canada with his dad and Chuck. He likens this area of Argentina to the prairie pothole region of the North American plains. He works his two duck calls like an old pro. He uses a single or double reed mallard call and creates a 'guttural slur' to bring in the rosy bills. Alternatively, he uses a pintail whistle-tweak, tweak-tweak ending in widgeon whistle chatter.

Chuck is a great guy. We have shot francolin over pointers in the Orange Free State of South Africa, dove streaming into sunflowers near Kimberley, and driven guinea fowl near Sun City. Add to this the geese, partridge and pigeon of a Bahia Blanca, dove in Cordoba province, and now the duck shooting just south of Buenos Aires. Amazing considering we first met only two months before this adventure.

The area is vast and lightly hunted. Brian guesses that there are fewer than a hundred hunters shooting the entire area. The first duck came in, a trio of rosy billed porchard, the most common species, when it was still too dark to shoot. Soon, as the sun slowly rose, the action became fast and furious. Duck came in singly, in pairs, trios, quartets, quintets; sometimes larger flocks, and sometimes two separate groups coming in almost simultaneously. It was July, winter in the Southern Hemisphere. Close to freezing, skim ice glazed the surface. The shooting kept us warm.

Sixty per cent of the ducks are rosy bills, thirty per cent are pintail and the remaining ten per cent comprised thirteen different species. The rosy bill has a clear membranous eyelid through which it can see under water. During our five shoots (three mornings and two afternoons) we bagged eleven different species. For collectors the complete list is as follows: speckled teal; Brazilian duck; Argentine blue-bill; silver teal; ringed teal; cinnamon teal; red shoveler; white cheeked pintail; yellow billed pintail; Chilean widgeon; white faced whistling duck; fulvous whistling duck; and rosy bill. (Four non sporting species of birds are visually intriguing. Two are raptors – the crested Cara Cara and the chimango. The Gara is almost turkey size. The tero or southern lapwing is also worth noting for birders.)

Chuck was quick and accurate with his autoloader and often had three or more ducks out of each flight. I was limited to a maximum of two shots with my trusty Perazzi over-under. I had some old, lead duck loads from Federal and Winchester that I brought down to use. Although the shells must have been twenty years old, they worked flawlessly. And no matter how much we shot, the ducks just kept pouring in. We had a self-imposed limit of 125 cartridges per man; we were all empty by 9:00 am.

Something I find interesting is the different views that civilized countries have on what is and is not fair chase or good sport. In the UK, for example, it is illegal to crate and shoot birds. While really designed as part of the ban on boxed pigeon shoots, it now makes tower releases illegal. (While British shooters cringe at the idea of tower releases, it is common and often done in a sporting manner in North America.) Yet British sportsmen have no qualms about night-flighting ducks or feeding ponds, both of which are considered unsporting and illegal in North America. Personally, I have no problem with either. Indeed, I will jump at the opportunity to shoot boxed pigeons in the rings of Spain or the USA.

Argentina has obviously been more influenced by the European sensibility as baiting is both legal and integral to the process. Each of the thirty ponds shot is fed 100 lbs of corn every two days, starting six weeks before the season. It is why the ducks favour the ponds of the ranches that the estate Los Patos controls.

Claudio Villaba, the head guide, 'thinks more like a duck than anyone I have ever met' say all who know him. He works very, very hard scouting, feeding, and planning. It all pays off as great shooting for guests. (Although correctly called clients, everyone works so hard making clients feel at home that no one really feels like merely paying guests.) His Labs, Red, the older dog, and Yellow, the youngster, work really well.

Los Patos is owned by Angel Lainez. Educated at an English preparatory school in Argentina and a publisher by profession, he is a charming, worldly man. Recently married to the lovely Lilly, he is very content living in Monte. Lilly kept pushing the local drink – Lemoncello – served chilled the way a Russian serves vodka. It is quite popular and delicious to those with a sweet tooth but a bit over the top for my palate.

The farmhouse has a main room focused around a fireplace. The dining room is ample for the shooting party. Four bedrooms, each with its own bath, are set for double occupancy.

The estate, with its sycamore and willow trees, is picturesque. Row on row of poplars were planted with Germanic precision by Angel to be sold at an appropriate moment as veneer.

A decoyed duck is a decoyed duck. Most of the birds decoyed well, except at one point when yours truly was more concerned with getting photographs than staying hidden. Some pass shooting was required, but with a couple of exceptions range was not excessive and 'sky busting' was never an issue. The afternoon sessions tended to provide taller duck.

The estate is less than an hour from the international airport, which means one can get a morning duck and afternoon perdiz shoot in with time for a shower before heading for the flight back.

As I get older, I tend to ask myself two questions before recommending a shoot. The first is what I would change. In this case, the answer was nothing. The second is would I do this trip again. Answer: in a heartbeat. I guess that says it all.

Dove in Cordoba

While I love all aspects of our shooting sport, sometimes I think I work too hard at having fun. Certainly the amazingly long haul to Argentina falls into this category. Too often trips are planned to arrive in Buenos Aires, switch airports to take another flight to Cordoba, drive directly from Cordoba to the dove fields, and start banging away. Indeed, most packages in Argentina are based around an afternoon arrival and shoot, two or three full days' of shooting, a morning shoot and then departure back to Buenos Aires. I am getting too old for this sort of schedule. Personally, it makes much more sense to spend a day or two in Buenos Aires, a great city, to recover from jetlag, and then go on to the shoot. I also feel that Argentina is too far to go for merely three days of shooting. To my mind it makes much sense to combine a dove shoot in Cordoba with a few days of duck shooting; some of the best wild duck shooting in the world can be found just south of Buenos Aires, in Bahia Blanca, and nearby in Uruguay.

I have travelled often to the Argentine. My first trip was in 1980 to write a story on trout fishing in Patagonia for *Town and Country* magazine. I made two more trips in the mid and late eighties for an addiction as great as any I've contracted save African safaris and extremely challenging driven birds – namely polo. For many years I would go to Colombia to pursue the same bird as found in Argentina – the eared dove. After all, it was only a shortish flight from Miami to Cali, Columbia. I would shoot with Jose Herrera, a great gent whose brother was the Governor of the province. Because of his political connections he would pick up shooters and whisk them through customs and immigration at lightening speed. Depending on the time of the year and the location of the doves, one would either shoot near Cali or travel to Buga and the hotel all shooters stayed at was the Guadalajara.

Then one year Jose called. 'Alex it is just too dangerous, I'm closing down.' To me, it always seemed like Argentina was too far to travel to shoot birds, brother was I wrong.

Cordoba was actually founded before Buenos Aires in the early 1600s and it boasts over 120 ancient churches, plus historic squares, charming restaurants and good shopping to amuse non shooting companions.

To say that the area is teeming with doves is to understate the obvious. Depending on which expert one believes, estimates vary from thirty to fifty-five million birds. This is a pest of significant proportions to farmers as dove breed three to four times a year and lay a couple of eggs each time. I was told seventy-five per cent of the hatch survives to adulthood and at about forty-five days old they fly off as adult birds, creating sport for shooters and a nightmare for Argentine agriculture. Zero population growth, regardless of the number of shooters present, just is not possible. At the lodge at which I was staying, Manuel Lainez's clients shoot in excess of ten million cartridges per year.

There are four main roosts in the area: Rio Ceballos, Santa Catalina, Macha and Churqui Canada. These are home to most of the birds in this section of Cordoba and in our three days of shooting we concentrated on the latter two.

We shot the foothills of Macha with scrub thorn bush and cactus, which was very reminiscent of the American Southwest. The tightness in my back, caused decades ago by a car crash, was exacerbated by a long, chartered plane trip from Bahia Blanca and my shooting suffered.

I am, or so it seems, used to shooting extremely long, extremely fast targets – tall driven pheasants and that wonderful bird, the European wood pigeon. Perhaps because these dove are so small I initially read the targets as being much further away than they actually were. The diminutive size of the eared dove creates the perception of great distance. At first I could not shoot my way out of a brown paper bag. When I cut my lead by sixty to eighty per cent the birds started to hit the ground with great consistency.

Dove shooting in South America is one of the great shooting schools of the world. One beauty of this sport is the variety of shots presented. The other is the great number of shots that one will take in a day. The typical shooter who comes to these lodges averages thirty-six boxes for each day of shooting. That is nearly a thousand cartridges. This provides tremendous practice at many different angles and at many different distances.

And with the shooting comes a Pavlovian feed whistle in the form of the noise associated with shotgunning, which brings in the scavengers from near and far. First to arrive are the large brown eagles. Drawn by the shooting, they seem to know that they are protected and perch near the shooters with imperious immunity. They seem to prefer cripples. Whether this is because they are drawn to the movements or enjoy their meat rare I cannot say. Often they gorged to the point of almost being unable to fly. They are not the only scavenger drawn to the shooting. Sheep come and eat the crops, goats prefer to eat the head and the crop, and the hogs that are also attracted to the shooting eat everything. With the plethora of scavengers about it is not surprising that the dove prefer to roost in Piquilla trees, the thorns of which keep most predators at bay.

While we are not scavengers, we are predators, indeed the animal at the very top of the food chain. We are here in July at the very height of their winter. Mid June to mid August are the cool months, although it is rarely cold. At 700 metres the climate is almost Mediterranean. And even when it is cold at night, the warm northern wind turns midday to shirtsleeves weather.

Climate plays an important part in the shooting experience. The rainy season runs between the end of November or early December until February or March. I have been told that most of the rain is at night so it does not interfere too much with the shooting. Mid August and September are spring months and this spring extends until late October. November is warmer still while December and January and part of February tend to be quite hot though it is a dry heat.

During their summer months the plan is to shoot early, have a siesta and then shoot again late from about 4:00 pm until 8 or 9 in the evening. From the beginning of July until the end of March the birds are concentrated in the hills. In early April they come in on corn; corn and sunflowers are the most important crops. One shoots the crops early in the morning. In a dry year one concentrates on the water holes during midday and pass shoots the doves late as they return to roost in the evening.

A large part of success has to do with scouting the various areas. All professionals in Argentina are expert at this.

Manuel lives at La Aguada, which is a five-bedroom lodge in the town of Villa Del Tortoral. Recently and purposely built, this compound includes a large living room with a roaring fireplace, a well stocked open bar, and an adjacent dining room. The food was outstanding and a good variety served by two white-glove butlers. A stone bridge over a small stream runs from the private bedrooms to this dining area. Rooms are all en suite, spacious and comfortable. All in all this is one of the best lodges that I have visited anywhere. And while it is newly built, old traditional windows and doors were found and purchased and installed to make it feel like an old *estancia* of the region.

Six miles away is their flagship and original lodge called Posta Del Norte. Originally it was an old stagecoach stop but it has been completely refurbished and built out and now boasts seven bedrooms, each with its own fireplace and bathroom. Service is similar in both, in other words outstanding, and both are kept immaculately clean. Octavo Crespo, Manuel's partner, runs this shoot and this house. One of the true beauties of both lodges is that as long as there are four shooters in the party, one can have the house exclusively for one's own group. This means that each shooter has his own private room and bath. I find this a big plus as I actually hate sharing with a stranger as no doubt one or both of us will snore.

From January through March, shooting can be combined with trout fishing in Patagonia or Golden Dorado fishing. All gauges including .410 are available. If I were to shoot this again with my 12-gauge gun I would pre-order very light 24-gram (⅞th ounce) loads. Doves do not take a lot of killing as they are very small birds. This is the ideal sport for shooting 20-gauge or even 28-gauge guns. Because of the high volume of cartridges shot, this is actually one of the few shoots where I would opt for an autoloader over a fixed breech gun unless I were shooting a 28 or .410. They do have shotguns for rent; both Berettas and Benellis, which they feel are the only guns reliable enough to handle the thousands of rounds put through them on a daily basis.

While all three days of dove shooting was memorable, and each day was very different from the others, it was the second day shooting in the hills of the roost known as Churqui Canada, located north of a lodge, which was my favourite. The birds went out low on a strong southern wind and came back quite high. And while Some Like It Hot, I prefer my birds tall. It was with these tall doves returning to roost that I really connected.

Standing at the top of the hill with the trees behind to break up my silhouette gave me good natural camouflage so the birds rarely flared; they did manoeuvre to their normal zigzagging pattern as they flew. After each box of shells, I would take a break and drink some water from the cooler that the bird boy carried. In addition to carrying the shells, soft drinks, and a clicker for keeping track both of birds killed and shots fired, these amiable, hard-working lads would pick up the birds like non-slip retrievers. They were also very good at keeping a fresh and endless supply of shells in one's pouch.

I carried only one gun with me on this trip, a 12-gauge Perazzi, which was definitely too much gun for the dove, but perfect for the duck and geese that we also shot in other regions. Not to beat myself up too much with recoil, I limited myself to 250 cartridges a morning and the same in the afternoon. If one were content not shooting at the tallest birds, a tightly choked .410 would also provide a great sport at moderate targets (one can kill a long way with a 28-gauge).

Excluding airfare, tips, and cartridges, the entire trip should set one back about £1,200 (sterling). This is a lot of bang for the buck, but do realize that it is easy to get caught up in the moment and shoot hundreds of boxes on a trip. Cartridges here are expensive, perhaps £5 (sterling) or US$10 a box, so the cost of cartridges can actually exceed the basic cost of the trip.

Another great lodge often reviewed in the magazines is Los Chanares. Now under new management it is even better. (Because they only shoot one roost they close in April and May when the shooting is not at its peak at the *estancia*.) The beauty of this lodge is that a long drive is five to ten minutes *within* the estate. One can sometimes shoot within walking distance of your bedroom.

Estancia Los Chanares is one of the best dove shooting lodges, perhaps the top destination in Argentina.

David Perez the owner states:

Our 7,000 acres of private property is the site of Macha, the largest dove roost in Argentina, with millions of doves roosting on or flying over our property at any given moment. There is nowhere else in the world that one can experience this calibre of dove shooting in a luxury five-star Spanish colonial-style lodge

He continues:

In 2000, Estancia Los Chanares was built with one key competitive advantage in mind: the largest roost in Cordoba is located inside our property, within a two-minute drive from the lodge. Because of this advantage most shooting grounds surround the property between the lodge and roost – many within a five-minute drive from the main house. There are no long drives and no achy bodies – except sore shoulders for high volume shooters. Shooters have time to relax and enjoy five-star lunches at the lodge, an afternoon siesta, a refreshing swim in the pool or a revitalizing massage.

Serge Dompierre, the previous owner of Los Chanares, developed a game management programme that included food crops inside the property – hundreds of acres of planted sunflower, wheat and sorghum.

In addition, Los Chanares was developed as a 'European-style shoot'. There are over 400 shooting stands from twenty-yard incoming shots for beginners to high forty-five to fifty-yard driven and crossing-type shots for top Guns. Wood pigeon, which provides good sport from June to October, is about an hour or so from the lodge. Activities for non-shooting companions include the pool, massage, a city tour and horseback riding.

The deluxe accommodations at Los Chanares are of the highest quality. Los Chanares recently underwent an expansion bringing the number of private suites to ten. The new suites are double occupancy with private bathrooms. Guests will enjoy gourmet three-course meals, the finest selection of Argentinean wines, and even authentic Cuban cigars are included in the price. The friendly Los Chanares staff has a 'can-do' attitude, making it a vibrant and fun place to visit. 'More recently, however, our reputation for outstanding quality of food and accommodations has been a major attracting factor for our guests.'

The estancia is located about seventy miles north of Cordoba, a comfortable hour and a quarter drive.

Colombia

Here, eared doves dominate the sky from first light till last and shooting 2,000 shells a day is common. (Note: Dove shooting, indeed travel, became too dangerous in the mid 1980s and I have not been back since. I preferred it to Argentina as travel time was much less. I include this chapter as the problems cannot continue forever, though I may not live long enough to see that day.)

Much is touted as 'the best in the world' these days. In reality, little is. However, the eared dove shooting in Colombia, South America, is undoubtedly some of the best dove shooting in the world. Quite frankly, the shooting is so good that it is difficult to describe to anyone who has not experienced it, as they simply can't comprehend what you are talking about.

Imagine a place where the doves dominate the sky from first light till last with virtually no letup – a place where you are almost limiting your shots to shoot, figuratively, a ton of shells in a day, and where you can, in fact, shoot many more cases a day if you want to; a place where the doves present some easy shots flying into the wind at thirty yards, or dramatically difficult shots when flying with the wind at fifty yards.

The doves are constantly moving, thereby giving gunners unlimited shooting. Also, shooters of all levels will enjoy the sport: hotshots will be challenged by the exceptionally high-flying birds travelling downwind at incredible speeds, while the less talented can pick targets at modest range.

In the 1980s, shooting in Cauca Valley, I averaged 1,000 shells a day while going only for the most distant shootable doves; many gunners in our groups burned twice that number. It may sound like a lot of shells and huge bag limits, but the paying sportsman is actually assisting with the conservation of the doves in Colombia. The millions of doves (estimates range into the millions) eat twenty per cent of the grain production. If sportsmen did not kill the number of doves they do, the farmers would be forced to poison the fields, which would only serve to destroy the dove population rather than control it.

To get to Cauca Valley, you must fly to Cali, Colombia, a three-hour hop from Miami. Once there you will be met by your outfitter, in my case, Jose Herrera of Hunting and Fishing in Colombia.

Only one gun per shooter was permitted to be brought into Colombia. I used a 12-gauge K-80 with 20-gauge titanium tubes and screw-in-chokes. Not only did it fulfil the legal requirements, but it gave me two gauges to choose from. You are also not allowed to bring your own ammunition into the country. The government, specifically the army, has a monopoly on all ammunition, and the shells available are okay, but expensive at $10 a box.

You will either stay at the Intercontinental Hotel in Cali (nice, modern with a wonderful swimming pool) or the Guadalajara Hotel in Buga (charming, old-fashioned with a wonderful swimming pool) – the location varies according to where the birds are.

Hot shots and less talented shots alike will find the dove shooting in Colombia extraordinary.

Wildfowling can sometimes offer additional sport on safari.
(© Gamebirds 2000 world copyrights)

While the shooter shows classic Percy Stanbury style he seems to be completely weighted down with binoculars and cartridges. It makes my back ache just watching him.
(© Gamebirds 2000 world copyrights)

Driven birds often come in density. Driving birds in Africa requires exceptionally large beating teams often over one hundred strong.

(© Gamebirds 2000 world copyrights)

Wild guinea fowl often prefer to run than fly. When they are pushed into the air they provide superb sport. While they are not archangels, they appear so large as to be almost intimidating.

(© Gamebirds 2000 world copyrights)

The typical
Spanish
architecture of
Los Chanares
recently up-
graded and
renovated
provides de luxe
accommodation
and (*right*) the
gun rack.
(*Los Chanares*)

From North America to the southern tip of South America to South Africa, indeed wherever there are dove, they are drawn to sunflowers.
(Los Chanares)

20-gauge autoloaders come into their own when hundreds and even thousands of shots per day are probable.
(Los Chanares)

La Cuesta with its fourteen bedrooms, fabulous food and stunning views of the Andalucian mountains, is situated in the midst of one of the world's great tall partridge shoots.
(Author)

The birds are so high at La Cuesta that amazingly this is one of the less intimidating drives – still it is challenge enough for any man or woman. We generally use this as a warm-up drive.
(Author)

A real sport will let the lesser birds fly by while trying to pluck the taller birds out of the sky. One must, however, select birds within the constraints of ability, choke and load. *(Author)*

This is a very typical traditional Spanish partridge shooting landscape which is often dotted with Spanish oak or olive trees. Note the blinds and pantallas plus secretario standing behind clicking.
(Author)

La Flamenca – partridge flying in the traditional way much like grouse going with the undulations of the terrain. If they are fast, as they are here, they provide testing sport.
(Author)

Often at the end of the day at Casa Sala the team gathers for a group photograph to put in the game book.
(Mr & Mrs Robert Hefner)

Standing on a floating blind, Badr Jafar put on an awesome display of wing shooting in Hungary.
(Author)

On the Continent it is customary for the birds to be laid out in orderly rows and columns. *(Author)*

Of the many areas that I shot in Morocco this was the only VIP tent; it was much appreciated as respite from the searing heat.
(Author)

Pierre Villiere was high gun on a number of outings in Morocco – his wife Susan and a local helper look on.
(Author)

Taking ducks coming in to decoys forty-five minutes from Buenos Aires.
(Author)

A fine retrieve among the decoys.
(Author)

Part VII – Africa

Rovos Rail's *The Pride of Africa*

Rolling out the red carpet is, actually, something I am used to. Hell – for years I lived in a castle. But even at Humewood, it is only in the figurative sense. On the Gamebirds Train Shoot Safari, with Rovos Rail's *The Pride of Africa*, it is quite literal. The train, bottle green and from the colonial era, comprises twelve carriages and is headed up by a Class 19D steam locomotive. Before passengers board, stewards serve champagne from silver ice buckets. We looked forward with keen anticipation to the African bush in winter by day and air-conditioned comfort by night. Not bad.

The shooting the next afternoon started shortly after *The Pride of Africa* stopped at a country siding. We Guns went off to walk up francolin on a nearby farm. In the evening, we returned and crowded into the observation bar. We were elated; adrenaline flowed.

Our timing coincided perfectly with the substantial flight of doves coming into a crop to feed. We enjoyed superb sport for the red-eyed subspecies, each hunter firing copious quantities of shells at forty-yard rockets.

Peter Johnson, whose brainchildren are the African Game Bird Research, Education and Development Trust and Rovos Rail Pride of African Train Shoot Safari, was our host. He smiled and reminded us that the best was still to come. Soon, we would be shooting driven guinea fowl and francolin – a completely unique experience. In Europe, the beating team normally consists of two dozen men and lads. In Africa, the beaters can often number more than 100, sometimes approaching 200. In addition, the line for the shooters often extends to nearly half a mile. Instead of Labs and Springers picking up fallen pheasant, grouse or partridge, 'bird boys' accomplish the task — quite similar, in fact, to those employed in places like Argentina.

Memories of Hunts Past

Most Gamebirds safaris are booked by a family or a team of friends. But occasionally, as with our trip, it is reserved by a party consisting primarily of strangers drawn together by a shared common interest. Even though most of us were initially strangers, camaraderie based on a shared passion quickly developed. The train headed north during the night then pulled off the main line at Kameel, a siding in North West Province. A stewardess woke us with coffee. After an early breakfast, we walked down a path beside the track.

Our host was Rod, who drove us up the Setlagole River Valley towards Nonen, Clober and the Kalahari bush country. At the top of a knoll stood a kudu bull, its grey sides glistening gold in the early morning light with its horns spiralling skyward. It made me think of all the kudu I have tracked, hunted and the few I chose to shoot. Waves of nostalgia wafted across my brain; I missed those days when I compulsively hunted Africa from one end to the other, always in search of the bigger trophy, the new land, the different experience. Those days have largely passed for me, but the memories linger.

The Drive at Nonen

We shot in an area called Nonen. Uniformed gunbearers and pickers-up, two to a Gun, awaited us. Each had the name of a Gun pinned to his chest. The feeling was very similar to a European driven shoot — yet different, as well. We drew pegs, as one would in Europe, and were assigned butts. We rotated from drive to drive and stood behind reed mats or screened butts spaced along fence lines, dry watercourses or farm tracks. These were not permanent. They were, however, reminiscent of those found on Spanish shoots for partridge — canvas butts put up for the day.

At that point, the usual, expected shoot speech was presented. Safety was paramount and the rules were gone over, from A to Z. Of course, ground game was taboo, as it is in most of Europe. It is just too dangerous for the beaters.

Two shots from the beating line announced the start of the drive, and a line of 120 farm workers, neatly clad in matching overalls, advanced in well-rehearsed precision — tapping the bush, beating it and waving flags. The birds could be driven the full distance, often half a mile, or could be holding in thickets only fifty yards from the line of guns, until forced to fly by the beaters. An unusual group of ground game did manage to work its way through the line: impala, kudu, warthog, duiker and steenbok, flushed by the beating team.

Helmeted guinea fowl streaked across the gun line, some singly, some in small flocks and in large flocks 100-strong. As with all driven shoots, blue sky must be seen *under* the bird to be safe. Two species of francolin, Orange River and Swainson's, flying faster than the guinea fowl, came straight to us, much more like partridge. They also offered crossing shots, which proved interesting and tricky. Again, as in Europe, a whistle sounded, and the drive was over as the beaters emerged through the thickets in front of us.

We returned to a ranch house and lunched on cold beef and salads. The house was built on the edge of a high knoll, where it could catch the cool breeze and from where we could overlook the broad valley expanding toward the low hills in the blue distance.

The shooting was even better in the afternoon. There were more species. Most guns resisted the four species of dove (red-eyed, turtle, Cape and laughing), having discovered that if you shoot too often at them, you will be reloading just at the instant seventy guinea fowl thunder overhead.

Dust over the distant Kalahari turned the sky a deep crimson as the day's bag was laid out in a clearing – fifteen rows of twenty. The beaters sang traditional warrior hunting songs and danced around the birds as darkness rushed in. (Bags on these shoots are not huge, high-volume affairs. All the game is wild, and unless you get into a good flight of dove, pigeon or sand grouse, the bags are moderate but more than sufficient for grand sport.)

The following day, the non-shooting companions in our party visited Tswalu Game Reserve. We went off to shoot driven guinea fowl, francolin and doves and the nearby 'papies'. On one of the drives, there was the exciting possibility that rooting warthogs might be disturbed and charge the length of the line, thereby scattering many of the Guns.

Later in the morning, we paused in the shade for some tea and homemade biscuits. For lunch, we returned to the house for good South African wine, delicious game and other local specialities, again cooked colonial style. The temptation for a siesta was strong but was overcome as we went out to hunt the edges of cultivated land. There, birds feed on sorghum, peanuts and corn crops. We found the afternoon shoot even better than it had been that morning.

The Last Drive

The last drive was exceptional. The Gun line lay at the foot of a small valley that curved around a hill. We heard the beaters coming up the far side and waited for the birds to be driven towards us. We were caught off guard when a flock of 100 guinea fowl, along with francolin and hundreds of doves, swung around one side of the hill and up the valley. The shooters in the first butts were too slow and still mounting their guns when those in the middle fired. Those at the upper end had the most warning and, consequently, got the best action. Nevertheless, it was not just the shooting; it was the spectacle – the bronze band of birds in the late light, slanting across the slope above us, held us spellbound.

By Trains and Planes

We slept like angels as the train moved south during the night. The next morning revealed a terrific flight of dove and pigeon. Later that day, we shot spurwing and Egyptian geese, in addition to plenty of red billed teal and yellow billed duck in harvested grain fields near the Vaal River. At the same time, wives and girlfriends flew by private charter to the diamond city of Kimberley for a tour.

Early the next morning, we used the same plane to fly to the Langberg Mountains, located in the heart of the Kalahari Desert. Shooting for Namaqua sand grouse flighting into water was superb. Set in this vast landscape was a series of waterholes known in this desert as 'pans'. Hendrick, our host for this shoot, had placed a dozen sunken butts into the ground in a circle around each of the many waterholes.

Sand grouse began to appear in small flocks. More and more flew by, until much of the western sky was constantly speckled by flocks of birds. A tailwind pushed them an extra thirty miles an hour, yielding fantastic sport. As abruptly as it started, it was over. We gathered our empty cartridge cases, picked up downed birds and headed for a drink and the spectacular picnic brunch for which Hendrick and his wife were famous. It had been a brilliant, elating morning of grand, classic sport.

We returned to the train and continued north past the Botswana border. Distant bush fires, common this time of year, raged. We arrived at our destination in northern Botswana. As we left the train in the early morning darkness, a biting wind hit us. We departed for a morning of flighted dove. This sort of weather is generally not the best type of hot-barrelled action we had in mind. However, the small waterhole in an otherwise dry riverbed with thorny scrub surrounding it looked ideal.

We were in our butts by 8.30 in the morning, but nothing happened. The staff, always confident and helpful, served hot tea and coffee to keep us in good humour. Soon, the wind died down, and the rush of doves began. We shot more than 300 and expended many times that number of cartridges.

Into Zambia

Late the next day, we crossed the Zambezi River over the famous Victoria Falls bridge. The train slowed to a stop, enabling us to get out and take spectacular pictures of the falls. We moved into Zambia from Livingstone for our last two days of driven shooting near Choma. The farm we were using for the shoot was situated well inland at one of the few places where the Zambezi could be forded in the old days. The farm was originally granted to a hunter named Walker in 1898 in exchange for showing the British South Africa Company where its troops could enter the country. It was then purchased by Paddy Bruce-Miller shortly after World War Two.

From the siding, we drove to the farm. One hundred and fifty Tsonga beaters welcomed us near the main gate and burst into tribal song and dance. Paddy's son, Ian, his family and friends greeted us with an African high tea. Our companions then flew off for a day of sightseeing on the Zambezi; we headed off to shoot.

Our destination was the Miombo woodland beyond the bright canna and strelizia beds on the perimeter of the well-watered garden. There, we enjoyed two of the finest days of driven shooting that we experienced on this trip (and, we were told, two of the best driven days that Africa had to offer). We were rewarded with guinea fowl, five species of francolin (Swainson's, Natal, crested, rednecked and Shelley's), four species of pigeon, dove and an occasional quail, as well. Somehow, we accomplished a remarkable twenty drives in two days – each different – each providing spectacular challenges or prolific sport.

The trip lasted nine days. We enjoyed six days of superb sport and returned with many memories to carry us through the Northern Hemisphere's cold winter. We returned to the train for the last time, taking the short run back to Victoria Falls.

Peter Johnson

Peter Johnson, born in Rhodesia and educated in England, is one of the world's premier wildlife photographers. He has shot most of his life and is a traditional sportsman and conservationist – in the best sense of the terms. Early in his career, Johnson realized that farmland was the best place to increase the wild population of game. He believed that farmers would manage their land for wildlife rather than for domestic breeds if it showed profit.

Johnson founded the African Gamebird Research, Education and Development Trust (AGRED) to scientifically research and investigate the feasibility of managing habitat for increased game bird production in various parts of Southern Africa. He then formed Gamebirds Southern Africa to market the harvesting of game birds as a profitable by-product to agriculture as a sustainable source of income. All the private properties we were to shoot are members of this unique association and have applied the research and implemented the wildlife management recommendations successfully. Today the Gamebirds association represents well over two million acres of privately owned estates, stretching from Cape Town to the Tanzania border.

Johnson explained:

Good wild bird shooting is the result of good conservation and good conservation is good business. It is not only the wild bird numbers that have increased. There is also more wildlife of many kinds, from leopards to field mice, due to the new style of management – so much so that fifty members of our association now contribute to the restocking of wildlife areas where it has disappeared, through annual live game captured on their estates and then translocation and sale to areas of paucity.

Gamebirds Train Shoot Safari

From the moment one arrives at the train station until the safari is over, virtually everything is included, such as cartridges, air charters, guides, licences, laundry, game park fees, etc. Excluded items include cartridges other than 12- or 20-gauge, antelope shoots, taxidermy and telephone calls.

The shooting season runs from 1 June to 31 September, although the normal train-shoot safari runs from the third week of June through to the first ten days of September.

Various itineraries are offered, varying in length from six to nine days. Most itineraries average five or six days of shooting. Different legs take one through South Africa from Pretoria through Botswana through Victoria Falls, or from Victoria Falls north to the Tanzanian border.

The cost of the shoot varies with the itinerary and the size of the group. The minimum number of shooters is eight; the price drops when there are ten Guns in the party and again if the party is filled to twelve (ten Guns are the maximum for the Tanzania trip). Larger 'royal suites' are available for an extra charge. However, the 'average' room is quite luxurious. There are some details to keep in mind. It can take quite some time to organize visas for Zambia, so allow sufficient time. In addition, remember that malaria prophylaxis and other obvious vaccinations must also be taken care of. Antelope shooting can be organized on most trips with advance notice – and at additional cost.

Kenya

Kenya, always the top choice of sportsmen, has re-opened its doors to bird shooting. You can go on a deluxe, tented safari and experience Africa as it should be experienced.

From the earliest organized safari days to 1976–7, Kenya attracted the lion's share of sportsmen, even after the introduction of the aircraft made other parts of Africa more accessible. The early safaris were by horse, ox cart and foot and one of the first questions likely to be posed by the white hunter to his client was 'Can you walk?' Kenya was the first choice for a number of reasons – relatively easy access by ship from Europe, a healthy climate by African standards, and a wide variety of sporting opportunities.

One must remember that lion, rhino and other prized trophies were considered pests and treated like vermin during the early 1900s (see John Hunter's book *Hunter*, out of print but easy to find and cheap). The adventurous hunted bongo under difficult and very sporting conditions or went after the huge lion and buffalo.

In 1976 Kenya banned elephant hunting and then shut down all hunting in 1977, primarily to cover up illegal poaching of ivory and rhino condoned by the government. Within a month of closure, rumours starting flying that Kenya would re-open; they have been flying ever since. (At the 1981 Game Coin Convention, a biennial event held in San Antonio, which every sportsman would enjoy, one of the deans of the East African Hunters, Tony Dyer, said that he would believe it only when it happened.) This is still true: big game is not open in Kenya, and nobody knows when it will be.

The big news in the mid 1980s, however, was that bird shooting was re-opened in Kenya. Closed since 1977, the opportunity for first-class sport now exists. Prices include everything except ammunition, licences, shooting block fees and champagne. For less than a first-class shoot in Great Britain or Spain, one can not only experience fabulous bird shooting but can spend time viewing game from foot, horseback or vehicle. For about the same cost, trout and big game fishing can be added to the itinerary.

The Kenya Hunters Association was formed when bird shooting re-opened. All hunters are required to be members, and professionals must pass a test. Visitors can join on a temporary basis. While in New York, renowned hunter Tony Seth-Smith said that he felt it was an excellent move on the part of the government since hunting financially rewards the new African landowner for protecting game on his property.

Since itineraries are designed to specification, one can shoot many species in a day and, by changing locales, enjoy both upland and waterfowl shoots. In other words, camps can be moved. Exact season and bag limits seem to vary somewhat from year to year but include: francolin, spur fowl, guinea fowl, quail, partridge and lesser bustard. There are several types of francolin and three varieties of guinea fowl (occurring in large flocks). These are fun to drive. Lesser bustards can be found on the plains.

Kenya has many varieties of geese, ducks and teal, etc., and they are seasonal. The three types of sand grouse in Kenya flock into waterholes in the morning in large numbers, sometimes for several hours. There are several varieties of dove and pigeon, which also hit the waterholes and feeding grounds in their hundreds.

The shooting can be breathtakingly fast. Sand grouse (actually more closely related to a pigeon than a grouse, though the colouring is similar) can put on a show of aerial acrobatics that will challenge the best shooter. Guinea fowl are fairly easy targets. The francolin, which resembles a cross between a grouse and a hen pheasant, takes off with a burst of speed and is excellent sport.

A couple of my friends have said that Kenya is 'an awful long way to go to shoot birds'. Certainly, one can find great dove shooting in South America or even Texas. One can shoot grouse, geese or snipe closer to home, but one cannot get the variety of bird shooting offered in Africa anywhere else. And the African experience – the properly tented camp, the dinner under the stars, and the opportunity to view game – exists nowhere else on earth. This is a deluxe, tented safari, complete with a Land Rover and a professional for every four clients, where one is able to get off the beaten path and do exactly as one pleases A full staff is in tow on a safari lorry outfitted with camp equipment.

But more important than just the shooting and fishing, one will be on safari with a top operator in a magnificent land. Whether one travels to the Northern Frontier District, famous in the old days for big tuskers, or Masailand through which the great wildebeest migrations flow and where the elegant Masai still herd their cattle, or the Aberdares where the most sporting bongo hunting existed, one will be experiencing Africa as it should be experienced – not as part of a pre-packed tour stuffed like a sardine inside a VW bus. You really cannot do better. Tony Seth-Smith and Danny McCallum run excellent operations in East Africa.

Similar lodge or tented bird-shooting safaris are possible in Botswana, Tanzania, and Zambia.

The Road To Morocco –
A Cautionary Tale

My articles normally have a life of their own; the lead and the story are obvious. Pinos Altos (originally published in *Shooting Sportsman* in 2004) melded both thirty-year-old and new Spanish partridge experiences into a tapestry that, I hope, gives the reader a good overview of shooting in Spain. My recent reviews in the UK's *Shooting Gazette*, re-published and updated in this tome, both of Lord Carnarvon's Highclere (aka King Tut's shoot) and the Duke of Wellington's Stratfield Saye shoot had easy historic links.

Morocco has been more difficult.

I had recently signed a book deal on the world's best shoots. Few writers know the British Isles and continental Europe shoots better than I, having forty years' and nearly a thousand days' experience. Certainly a number of writers do know South America, or wildfowling, for example, better than I. I have shot woodcock, ruffed grouse, pheasant, quail and wildfowl in North America for forty-nine seasons, running my own English setters for twenty years. But the world is global (yes, I know that is a tautology) and I felt I needed to cover both the obvious, for example, Rovos Rail in Southern Africa and dove in Cordoba, and the somewhat more obscure, but potentially interesting and even intriguing, venues with which my familiarity was minimal. North Africa leapt to mind.

About twenty years ago, I shot Morocco, starting in Casablanca on a partridge and pheasant shoot. Unfortunately these were birds being released from crates and were completely without appeal. (The only interesting occurrence, if you could call it that, was a mirror falling off the wall in the bathroom for no apparent cause. This neatly sliced my leg for about six inches along the muscle below the knee. I called reception asking for a doctor, desperately needing stitches, explaining what happened. These geniuses of efficiency sent a plumber instead.

Only after pointing at my leg and speaking in, shall we say, slightly annoyed tonalities did the handyman grasp the situation well enough to call the front desk to explain that a doctor took precedence over the mirror.) A couple of days later we went up to a snipe and duck marsh near Tangiers where the wild bird shooting was very interesting – the biggest flights of tightly packed snipe that I've ever seen – and we also enjoyed a day of driven wild boar.

This shooting tour then headed down to Marrakesh where we stayed at the great, famous, La Mamounia, a slightly over the top hotel. The plan was to shoot wild partridge (Moroccan Barbarian partridge) found at about 1,000 feet, in the Atlas Mountains. But the trip had been so disappointing up to this time that I decided to bail and flew to the Isle of Lewis in the Outer Hebrides to shoot with a group of American friends who owned Garynahine estate at the time. (My friends on the Moroccan shoot told me after that the partridge were the highlight of the trip.)

For my second adventure to Morocco almost twenty years later, I contacted one of the biggest non-American, and generally accepted as one of the best, booking agencies to arrange this expedition.

The dove season in Morocco used to take place in May when the weather was generally pleasant. Now the main season runs from mid June to mid July when it is hot enough to fry eggs on the sidewalk. (I say main, because it is legal through to 15 August, but few go at that time.) The agency insisted on booking flights for me from Dublin (where I was based) to London – London to Casablanca – Casablanca to Agadir; then driving to Taroudant. This meant leaving my house at six in the morning and not arriving at the Gazelle D'Or, starved and exhausted, until after 2 am. If there is worse airline food than Air Morocco, I have never experienced it; and if there is any place more dangerous to eat fast food than the airport in Casablanca, one would have to go to the Sudan. What was really annoying was that there were direct flights, Dublin to Agadir, with the total travel time a non-stop three and a half hours. The other annoying factor was that the itinerary forced upon me cost four times as much as the direct charter. The agency claimed that it only worked if I travelled with a group – there was no group, just one other sportsman – but when I asked the owner of the Moroccan company and their representatives, they said they would have met me regardless of which flight I took.

Before I go any further, I must say that the Moroccan company itself is very well organized. The owner is a charming and intelligent man and his assistant, Frederique Hebrard, proved outstanding and would be an asset to any shooting company – she is organized, charming and helpful.

At the airport I met Pierre Villere, who would be my shooting companion for the duration, and his wife Susan. We hit it off and quickly became friends. I also ran into Carlos Rua who runs a good partridge operation near Madrid. Carlos is one of the most charming shoot hosts imaginable – small world.

One shoots in the early hours of the morning, departing the hotel by about 5 am and returning between 9 and 10 am. By the end of the morning session it is getting quite hot. The afternoon session centres on the last three or four hours of daylight and it is exceedingly hot throughout the period. Arriving after 2 in the morning, we were provided with a buffet of cold roast beef, but there was no way that I could wake up an hour later and head off shooting. In fact, it was so exhausting that I could hardly make it out to the next afternoon's session.

Frederique gave me an article written by Romi Perkins (part of the Orvis clan), describing how beautiful and pleasant it was staying at the Gazelle D'Or shooting in May with the temperature of 68 degrees. Early July pushed temperatures well over ninety and the room was not air-conditioned. Indeed, the mosquito screens for the windows had gaps and the major sport of my day was swatting mosquitoes before going to sleep. I believe the season starts later now than in Perkins' time because there are fewer doves. (The turtle doves are migratory.) A limit of fifty birds per day is now enforced and while I did reach that in a couple of sessions, most other shooters – using the same company – did not reach their limits. Bag limits on birds can be viewed in a number of ways. It is perfectly possible to go to Argentina and shoot hundreds or even thousands of birds a day or to go to a wild marsh in the Midwest and find a five duck limit thoroughly enjoyable. But since most shooters associate dove with high volume, a limit of fifty, often not reached, is not really the best option. I had hoped for sufficient sport to make travel from the British Isles worthwhile. It wasn't. It certainly is not if Mexico and South America are closer.

On two of the eight sessions, Pierre did shoot a couple of hundred rounds, which made him far away the most productive shooter. Some Guns shot only a box or two each session. I skipped the first morning and only shot one afternoon as I could not deal with the afternoon heat.

We stayed at the Gazelle D'or, once a beautiful oasis in a sea of sand. The original owners, I believe, have died off, and it is now in different hands. Unfortunately, the old Gazelle D'or ain't what she used to be. The staff were helpful and nice, especially the new manager, but that did not make up for a basic lack of hygiene. Renata got terrible food poisoning as did a contingent of a dozen Brits who we met flying out. The hotel played this down but did admit it happened… 'I wish I knew the cause,' stated the manager.

5 am came earlier than usual, or so it seemed. The owner of the company, Abdelmalek Laraichi, sits on the porch of the Gazelle D'Or holding court over his minions. He is here before 5 am when I arrive. He stops puffing on his Cohiba, gets up and greets me speaking very good English with a slightly British accent and French intonation. 'There are clouds in the sky. This will not be a very good day,' he confides. 'For good shooting you need blue skies. Perhaps it is the inability of the dove to navigate from the roost to the grain and return. Maybe they worry that by the time they find their way back another will have stolen their spot.' To my mind, this is a lot of cognitive ability ascribed to a bird's brain. The turtle dove is different from eared dove and mourning dove, he states, telling me in hushed tone that 'These are the only dove that truly migrate. They come here each year from Mali, Niger, etc. to breed. When the young are old enough to fly, they return to their home countries.'

A fleet of four-wheel-drive vehicles takes us to a different area to shoot for each session. Our driver thinks he is Michael Schumacher, passing donkeys, humans, bicyclists, and other vehicles at breakneck speed. Our guide, Abdelsamad Khiati, works very hard to make certain all goes well. (The company has twelve guides and constantly scouts for the best areas.)

Turtle doves fly well with more moves than an F-16. Abdel seems to have eagle eyes, seemingly spotting doves two miles off. He concurs that the best shooting takes place on bright windy days. He cautions, 'Move a finger and the dove she will see you and change direction.'

Young bird boys, more than are needed, wait anxiously for the chance of a few hours of work and a few dollars tip. The better-off kids ride bikes; some merely run after the vehicles. Some are useful and hardworking and some are fairly useless, but, in all cases, one's heart breaks to see the poverty. We shoot near the Atlas Mountains – at least within view, both the High Atlas and the Ante Atlas. There are wild partridge, the Barbarian species, in the Atlas Mountains and this company can organize driven days for about 400 birds. There is also a wood pigeon that I did not see, but it is reported to be almost black. One tends to shoot dove near sugar cane and maize-like crops and a lot of watermelons litter the fields. Since the fields are also littered with donkey by-products, conceptually, I now prefer to wash my watermelons in boiling water before I eat them.

I have shot dove in Columbia, in Argentina, in Florida, in South Africa and in Morocco and all the different species of dove I have shot fly exceptionally well. Turtle dove make an interesting addition to a hunter's experience. Should the season return to May and should the Gazelle D'or – literally – return to its former glory, this would in theory be a very pleasant experience…But I would not hold my breath.

Signs

Signs in English and French are painted like cartoons stressing that one should not take low shots. This is actually very important as some sessions have pegs placed thirty yards from roads where bicyclists and donkey carts pass. Often one is near a hedge running perpendicular to the road, preventing one from seeing human traffic in advance of shooting. But paradox is not just a Gun: untrained bird boys will yell 'shoot, shoot, shoot!' even though to do so would be dangerous.

Seasons

The current season runs from 15 June to 15 August, four days per week, Friday to Monday, and is limited to thirty shooters with the company. October to December is partridge season; quail are walked up in February and March.

For this sort of shooting a good shoulder pad is helpful and safety glasses are a must. I wore a foreign legion-style hat to protect the back of my neck and gloves to prevent sunburn.

Part VIII – Caribbean

Casa de Campo – The World's Best Clay Pigeon Ground

I started going to Casa de Campo, near the town of La Romana on the south-eastern coast of the Dominican Republic, in the late 1970s for polo. It was one of the few places I could get into excellent medium-goal matches by renting horses for the game. The Maharajah Jabar Singh, a famous player and excellent coach, did a great job of running the club and producing professional polo players. In those days the 7,000-acre resort was owned by Gulf & Western and was the favourite toy of the company's colourful chairman, Charlie Bludhorn.

When I returned to the resort in the early 1980s I spent a good amount of time on the 245-acre Shooting Centre.

One day I noticed a flyer shoot underway in the pigeon ring. I went over and introduced myself and was invited to join in. That was my first meeting with the resort's new owner, Pepe Fanjul, whose devotion to the shooting sports is known on many continents.

Fanjul's pet project was to create a complete shooting facility. Today, Casa has not only the normal array of skeet, trap and wobble-trap layouts, but also two flyer rings with European Barnabee boxes. The sporting clays course (100-plus stations) is one of the best anywhere and provides challenging variations of each shot so the novice and expert alike can test their skills. Every April for the past two decades Casa has hosted the Sugar Invitational Shoot. The courses for these tournaments have presented relatively few long clays, yet most years only one or two shooters have managed scores in the 80s. This speaks much for the creativity of the original course designer/Shooting Centre director/shooting instructor Michael Rose, now retired but not forgotten.

'It took over two months to design the course at Casa de Campo,' Rose said. 'We had to do it via helicopter because the jungle was so thick we couldn't begin to see the potential by walking the grounds.'

The red-and-white high tower is the heart – and heartbreaker – of the course. It was built to withstand 150-mph hurricane winds and soars so far above the ground that it requires a light to ward off low-flying planes. Clays are thrown from forty, eighty and 110 feet. The most infuriating are launched from the top and approach directly overhead at extreme right and left angles. (The hard right is a forty-five- to sixty-yard target, depending on where it is taken and the vagaries of the wind.)

Rose is arguably the most famous bird-shooting coach of our time and, as former head instructor/gunfitter for Purdey's, taught many of the Royals to shoot. He is a short, fit man, with a strong English accent and a craggy face weathered by British wind and rain. Rental guns and ammunition are available at the Shooting Centre Pro Shop.

I have enjoyed extended stays at resorts from Gleneagles, in Scotland, to Sun City, in South Africa, but I know of no other that offers the shooting sportsman such an array of additional pursuits: three world-class golf courses, tennis (with ball boys provided), polo, casual horseback rides on the beach, squash, a fitness centre, beautiful beaches, all the usual water sports, nine restaurants, an artist colony and all manner of accommodation from fully staffed (cook, butler, maid and so on) villas on the beach to simpler but still very nicely appointed hotel rooms, many with nearby swimming pools.

For more information on Casa de Campo, contact Premier World Marketing.

Appendix 1
Protocol For a Driven Pheasant Shoot

For those readers who have not participated in a driven shoot, here are a few tips. The rules of decorum and etiquette for a driven shoot have evolved over the last two centuries. Ethical, pragmatic, financial, legal, historical and safety factors have honed and polished the rules of behaviour for driven pheasant and they vary greatly with grouse and partridge shooting since the latter are low flying, though very fast birds.

* Show up on time. The line waits for no man and you will likely miss the first drive if you are late.
* Dress suitably. Never wear bright colours. A brown or green tweed hat is also advantageous. Birds will flare from a shining forehead.
* Follow the instructions of your host to the letter. Never leave your butt or peg, unless you have been so instructed by the organizer. If you are not sure of something, ask.
* Carry enough cartridges. One cannot get more during a drive. I have shot 150 shells on many a drive over the years and on one beat in England, if I had been two stands to my left I would have needed double that number.
* Some days one is always likely to be in the thick of the action. On others – though rare – it seems like one is never really in it. Smile and accept a poor draw graciously. It all averages out and soon you'll be in high gear.
* Safety is the prime consideration. Always wear safety glasses and hearing protectors. *Never* follow a bird through the line. *Never* follow a bird unless you can see sky under the bird. There may be beaters unseen on the ridge ahead and dog handlers behind.
* *Never* shoot any game on the ground unless requested to do so by the landowner. Fox are generally shot in Denmark and Spain because

they kill birds and eggs, but not in England where they provide sport for fox hunters.

* Try not to poach a neighbour's bird. Draw an imaginary line between the two of you. If you both shoot at the same time at the same bird, be magnanimous even if you brought it down.

* Talk as little and as quietly as possible while on the line and while walking into a drive. Do not slam doors!

* Listen for the signals that mark the beginning and end of a drive, normally a blast on the horn, though sometimes it can also be a whistle.

* If you feel your neighbour is shooting dangerously, let him know it firmly but politely or speak to the shoot manager.

* When trying to take a bird behind always point the gun to the heavens rather than swinging it through the line as you turn.

* Normally one draws pegs for a butt before the opening drive, and then increases the number by two for all the subsequent beats. In England the normal number is eight, in Spain, Ireland and Denmark it is ten to twelve, so an appropriate matrix must be used in arriving at one's calculation (i.e. on an English line, matrix eight, number six goes to eight, seven to one, eight to two, one to three and so on).

* The major emphasis is on sporting birds. Never hesitate to let the low bird or simply unsporting bird go by. Similarly it is good sport, assuming that you are a good enough shot, to try for the birds at the outer limits of your capabilities.

* While one counts grouse by the brace – 150½ brace would be 301 birds – pheasants are counted individually.

Appendix 2
Contact Details

www.casadecampo.com for resort and shooting

Morocco contact chasses.t@wanadoo.net.ma

First Shot Outfitter, PO Box 974, Coleman, TX, 76834; tele. 325-280-3676 (Mike); 325-280-3675 (Monica); 325-625-1671 (Lodge); email firstshothunts@aol.com.

Caroline Everett at The Ledges Inn, 30 Ledges Inn Lane, Doaktown, New Brunswick, Canada E9C 1A7; 506-365-1820, fax – 7138.

Long Island guides for ducks and geese:
Tom Cornecelli 631 874 8474
Barry Kanavy 516 785 7171
Red Oster – layout boats for diving ducks, sea duck, old squaw
631 567 0077; cell 631 834 0970.

Deerfield Guide Service: Duane Arnister 631 726 5889 or 516 446 2286.

Virtually all the other shoots worth contacting are booked through www.drivenshooting.com

Appendix 3
Recommended Reading

The Great Shoots by Brian Martin, Quiller (2007)

The Complete Guide to Wingshooting by Alex Brant, The Lyons Press (2005)

A Shooting Man's Creed by Sir Joseph Nickerson, Quiller (2004)

Any basic book on gunsmithing for shotguns – a little knowledge and a few spare parts (e.g. a spare handle for an autoloader's bolt) can save a trip.

Index